John Maskall

Artificial Fireworks - 1785

Volume 1

John Maskall

Artificial Fireworks - 1785
Volume 1

ISBN/EAN: 9783337256050

Printed in Europe, USA, Canada, Australia, Japan

Cover: Foto ©Andreas Hilbeck / pixelio.de

More available books at **www.hansebooks.com**

To Major
CONGREVE.
this First Volume
of
Artificial Fireworks,
is
humbly dedicated
by
his most obedient
devoted Servant
John Maskall
1785.

Artificial Fireworks.

Fruiloni Wheel.

The Wheel consists of Beech wood, having a nave and 12 Spokes, Viz.t 6 above and 6 below; the Spokes are glewed into the Nave, and are hollowed at the outward ends to receive the Cases; the Spokes are set so as to Form returning Angles.

Dimensions.

	Inc.s 10.ths
a b	1,25.
a c	5,00.
e f &c	1,75.
e g	1,56.
i k	0,50.
h i	1,56.
l m	0,312.
n o	0,437.
p i	1,00.
q u	0,437.
r s Brass thimble	0,50.
t d	0,75.

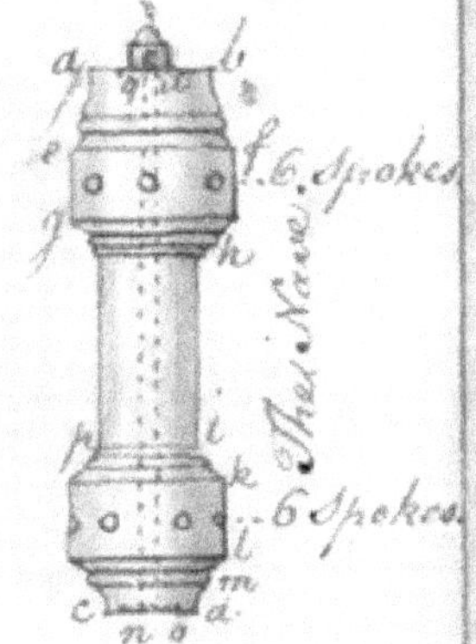

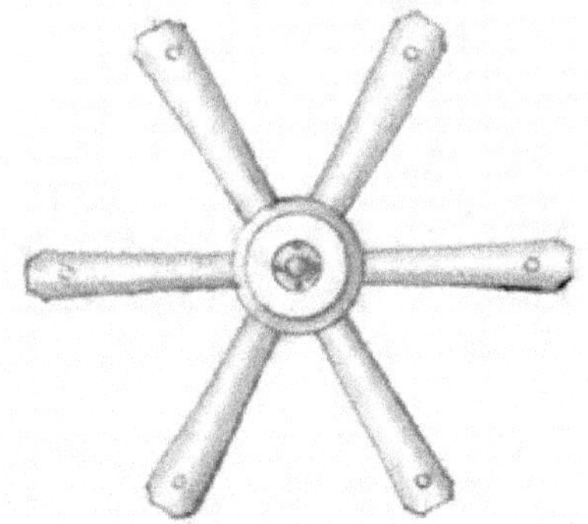

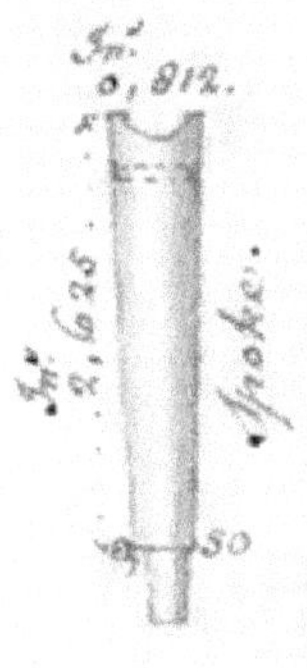

2

Fruiloni Wheel.

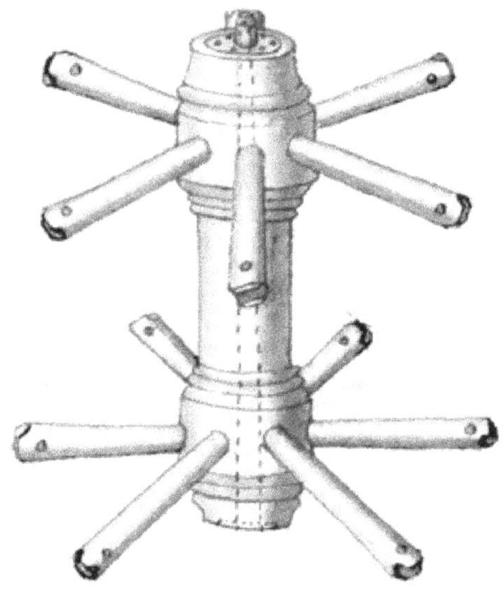

The Cases proper for this Wheel are those of two Ounces.

Whole Length of Case empty 6½ Ins.

Vent of Each Case equal to ⅓ of the diameter of the Bore.

All the Cases to be Markt to 5½ Ins exactly from the Choke end.

Each Case to have a button of brown paper stopt into the Vent which must be set up a little with a Mallet.

All Cases to be drove in the same Mould they were Rolled in.

To Prepare the Cases.

A Case being put into the Mould, first put in a 2 ounce ladlefull of Clay, then the iron drift and give 18 Strokes with an 8 Inch Mallet; then put in two ladlesfull of common fire and 21 strokes with the Mallet; Each to be prepared with one ladlefull of Clay and two ladlesfull of Common Fire exactly in the same manner.

It is proper to have a number of

Cases

Cases ready prepared in Store.

Common Fire for Preparing Cases.

	lb: oz.
Mealed Powder ————	1 : 0.
Salt Petre ————	0 : 4.
Sulphur ————	0 : 2.
Charcole ————	0 : 4.

To be first rubbed a little between the hands, then sifted four times through a hair Sieve and it will be fit for Use.

This Common Fire serves for Preparing all Cases.

Brilliant for 2 Ounce Cases.

	lb: oz: dr
Mealed Powder ————	1 : 4 :
Salt Petre ————	0 : 3.
Sulphur ————	0 : 1.
Iron Filings ————	0 : 3 : 8.

To be sifted four times through a hair Sieve, then to be well mixt by drawing it over with a brass Slice for 8 or 10 Minutes.

The Filings should be very clean and bright.

The

The Wheel requires 13 Cases, five of which must be dead heads, that is they must be Clayed above the Composition up to the Mark on the Case at 5½ Inches.

To drive the Brilliant. One 2 ounce ladlefull of Composition at a time and 18 Strikes to each ladlefull with an 8 Inch Mallet till the Case is drove up to the 6 Inches for which purpose the drift should be Marked: 8 of the Cases to be drove in this manner.

The five Cases for dead heads must likewise be drove with Brilliant; 4 of them to be drove to within ¼ of an inch of the Mark and then to have two ladlesfull of Clay drove upon the Brilliant; the 5.th Case to have only one ladlefull of Clay, because it is to go upon the Brass Nipple at top of the Wheel.

The Cases being drove and cut to the proper

proper length, must be bored at the Choke end with a Bit that is exactly the diameter of one third of the Bore of the Case, and to be Bored just through the Clay to touch the common-fire Composition; then the Cases to be primed with Quickmatch in short pieces, putting in one piece tight with a round pointed pricker, to keep the rest firm.

The Cases being Quickmatched must be Cartouched with tube paper to go just three times round the Case and tied on with coarse twine; the 5 dead heads are only to be Cartouched at the Choke end, and the others at both ends, to receive the leaders which are to communicate the fire.

It is necessary before the Cases are cartouched, to center each Case from end to end, that they may be placed and tied on even on the spokes.

The Wheel must be strung with coarse twine, put loose three times through

the

the hole of each Spoke to receive the Cases; the top Case must be fixed on the Nipple with two brads on each side well tied with coarse twine, then covered with pasted double tube paper pressed close; the other Cases may then be tied on the Spokes in the following Order; take any one of the Cases that is double Cartouched and beginning at any One of the lower Spokes, put the Case in between the hollow of the Spoke and the loose twine placing the middle of the Case in the middle of the Spoke, then pull the twine tight and secure it with a good knot; then another Case cartouched at each end must be placed and tied on to the next upper Spoke towards the left hand; then a dead head on the next upper Spoke; next three Cases double Cartouched following on the three next Spokes up and down; then a dead head; again three double Cartouched Cases and lastly two dead heads, one up one down; particularly observing to place the

the quickmatched end of all the Cases on the lower Spokes downwards; and the quickmatched end of all the top Cases, upwards.

In the next place all the strings round the Cases and about an inch on each spoke must be covered with paste tube paper doubled and pressed close; then set to dry.

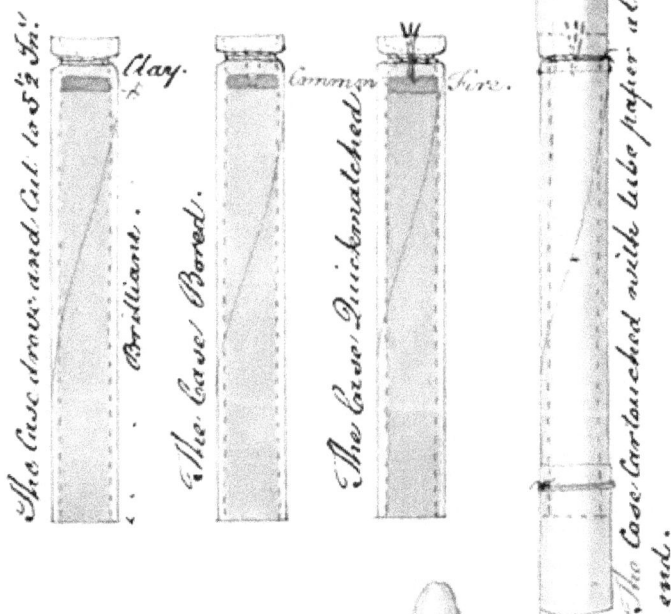

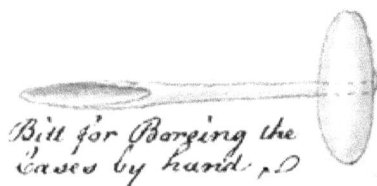

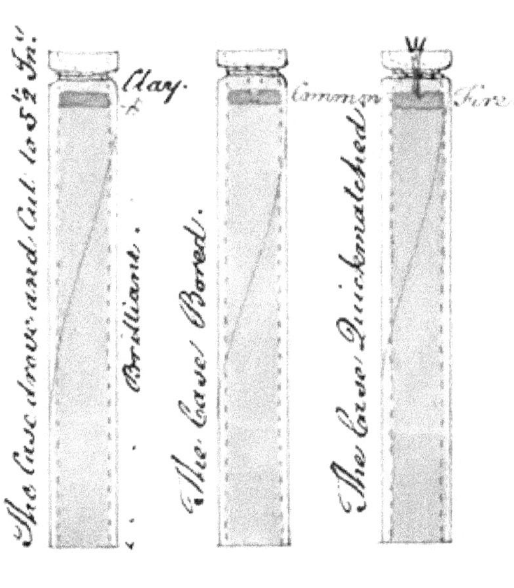

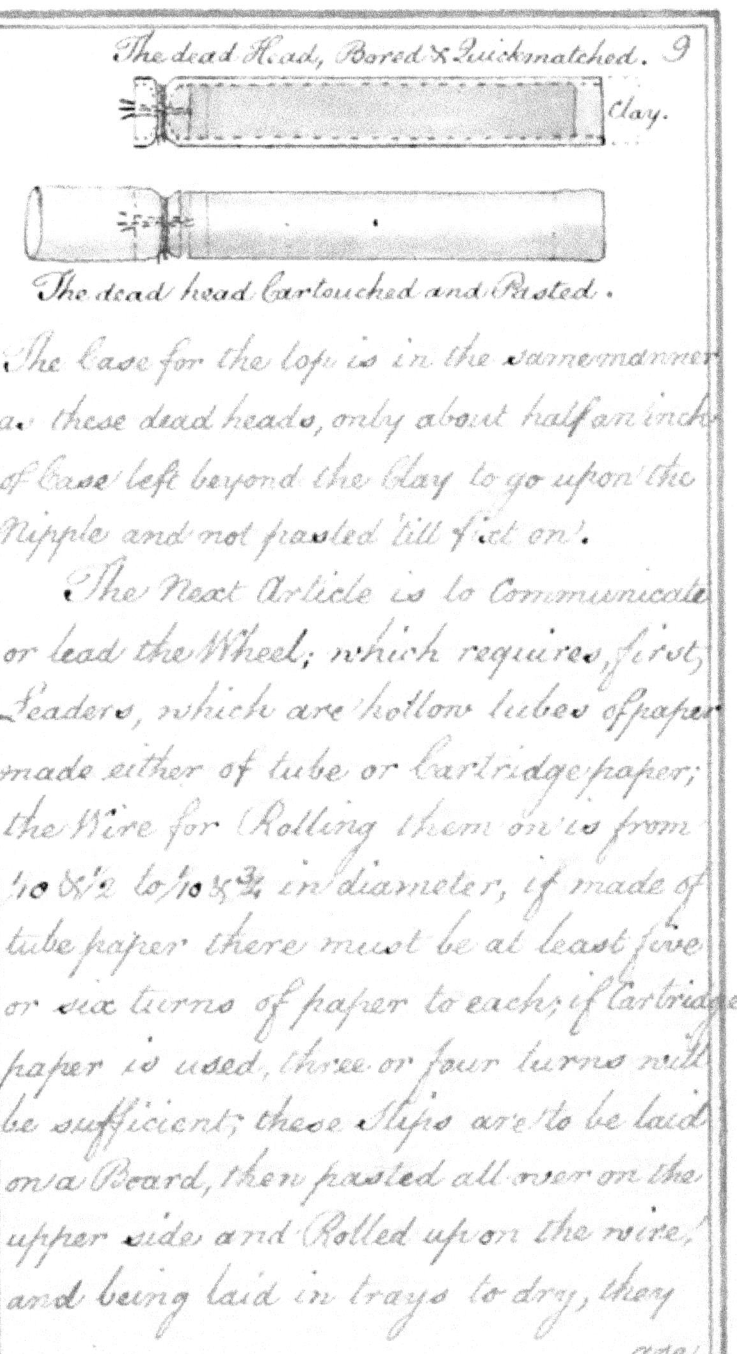

The dead head Cartouched and Pasted.

The Case for the top is in the same manner as these dead heads, only about half an inch of Case left beyond the Clay to go upon the Nipple and not pasted till fixt on.

The Next Article is to Communicate or lead the Wheel; which requires, first, Leaders, which are hollow tubes of paper made either of tube or Cartridge paper; the Wire for Rolling them on is from $\frac{1}{10}$ & $\frac{1}{2}$ to $\frac{1}{10}$ & $\frac{3}{4}$ in diameter, if made of tube paper there must be at least five or six turns of paper to each; if Cartridge paper is used, three or four turns will be sufficient; these Slips are to be laid on a Board, then pasted all over on the upper side and Rolled up on the wire, and being laid in trays to dry, they

are

are to be Compleated by dry Rolling them with a Rolling Board, Of these and other Leaders there should always be a sufficient Stock in readiness.

Cotton Quickmatch of three threads to be Used for filling and priming the Leaders.

I here beg leave to introduce a Scheme for Explaining the Method of communicating the Cases, deduced from the Circles of the lower and upper Spokes produced in length.

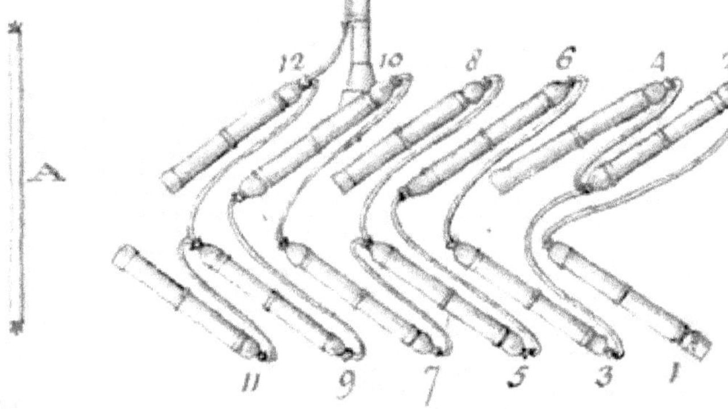

13
12 10 8 6 4 2
A
11 9 7 5 3 1

Explanation.

N.º 1. being the first Case is not to have a leader fixt to it till the Wheel

is

is put upon it's Stand for Firing.

No. 1 Communicates to No. 2; and No. 2 communicates to No. 3 and 4 which are both to Burn at the same time, one up the other down; but No. 4 is called a dead head because it does not communicate to any other Case after it is Burnt out; then No. 3 communicates to No. 6 and No. 6 to No. 5.

No. 5 communicates to No. 7 and 8 which both burn at the same time.

No. 7 communicates to No. 10 and No. 10 to No. 9.

No. 9 communicates to No. 11: 12 and 13, which three Cases are all to Burn at the same time and Conclude the Wheel.

A shews a leader properly Quickmatch'd, the Method is to take an empty leader and putting one end into the upper Cartouch of No. 1 produce it to the upper Cartouch of No. 2 allowing an inch or two more than will reach from Case to Case for turning, this is called Measuring, then the then the leader to be cut off at it's proper length, and a length of Quick-match put through and cut off at one end, put a short piece or two into each end, making room for them with a sharp pointed pricker then cut off the ends at about ¼ of an inch from each end of the leader.

To fix the leader, is only to put one end into the Cartouch of No. 1 so as to touch the Composition; then gathering the Cartouch together tie it round with two or three turns of coarse twine, and bending the leader carefully back bring the other end to the upper Cartouch of No. 2 putting Quickmatch to Quickmatch then gathering the Cartouch together tie it in as before; in like manner measuring, Cutting to the proper length, Quickmatching, Fixing and tying in the leaders from Case to Case according to the foregoing Scheme, observing not to tie in the leaders too hard, but only sufficient to keep them in the Cartouches, if tied too hard would probably stop the Communication, or produce a report from the Quickmatch being too much confined; lastly it must be pasted with double tube paper all over the Cartouches, a little over on each Case and a little over on the leader beyond the Cartouch, then set to dry.

Column with Iron Spindle.

The Fruitoni Wheel Fixt for Firing.

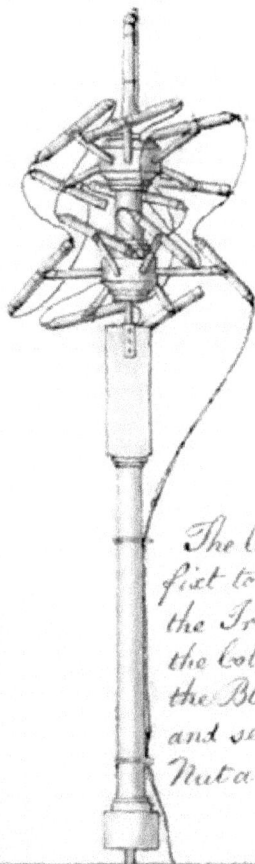

The Column is to be fixt to a common Triangle the Iron at bottom of the Column goes through the Block of the Triangle and secured by a large Nut and a Wrench.

Vertical Wheel.

These Wheels are likewise calculated for 2 Ounce Cases and are nearly of the same size as the Fruiloni, but the Block is not so long and the Spokes only turned so as just to clear the Cases and give room for Communicating, tying and pasting.

The Cases are the same as for the Fruiloni, Viz.t the Vent 1/3 of the Bore; the Vents to be stopped with paper; each Case to have one ladlefull of Clay drove in and two ladlesfull of Common Fire, which is called preparing them.

The Cases then to be drove with Brilliant exactly as before, the same Ladle, Mallet and number of Strokes to each ladlefull. Each Case when drove to be cut off at 5½ Inches; then to be Bored, Quickmatched and Cartouched at both ends, except one which must be a dead head and the finishing Case.

The Spokes of the Wheel to be strung with coarse twine, the Cases tied on and

pasted

pasted with double paper round the Case over the twine and a little over each spoke next the Case then set to dry, taking particular Care to place the Quickmatch'd end of each Case towards the right hand.

For Variety's sake, the Strong Yellow Fire composed of 1 lb of Mealed powder and 2½ Ounces of Golden Sand mixt together, may be drove in every third Case Exactly as the Brilliant, but it will be necessary to Mark these Cases to prevent mistakes in fixing them on the Wheel, then there will be two Cases of Brilliant and one of yellow in sequence.

The Number of Cases for this Wheel is 12 and they are to be regularly Communicated from Case to Case, that is, from the tail of the first Case in front (next to the dead head) to the Quickmatch'd end of the next Case behind

The measuring from Case to Case, cutting the leader to the proper length, quickmatching them, fixing and tying them in the Cartouches and pasting them afterwards is only one Method repeated.

But

But it will be proper to Observe, that if the Spokes are equally distant from each other and the Cases regularly tied on; one measurement will serve for all the 11 leaders, which may be all cut and prepared of an equal length.

The Spokes are the same Size as for the Bruilani Wheel; and one of these is strung with twine to shew the Method.

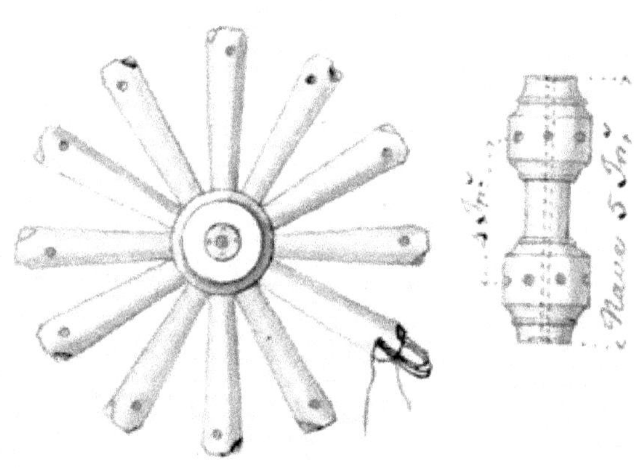

The Upper and Lower Circles produced.

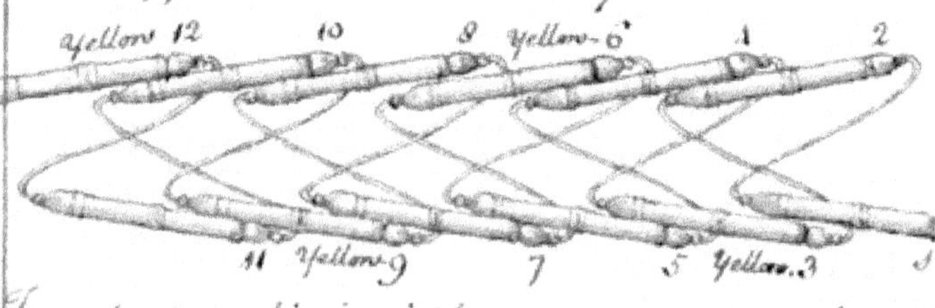

To understand this, it will be necessary to suppose the Wheel placed on a Block & Spindle, as is always done for Fixing.

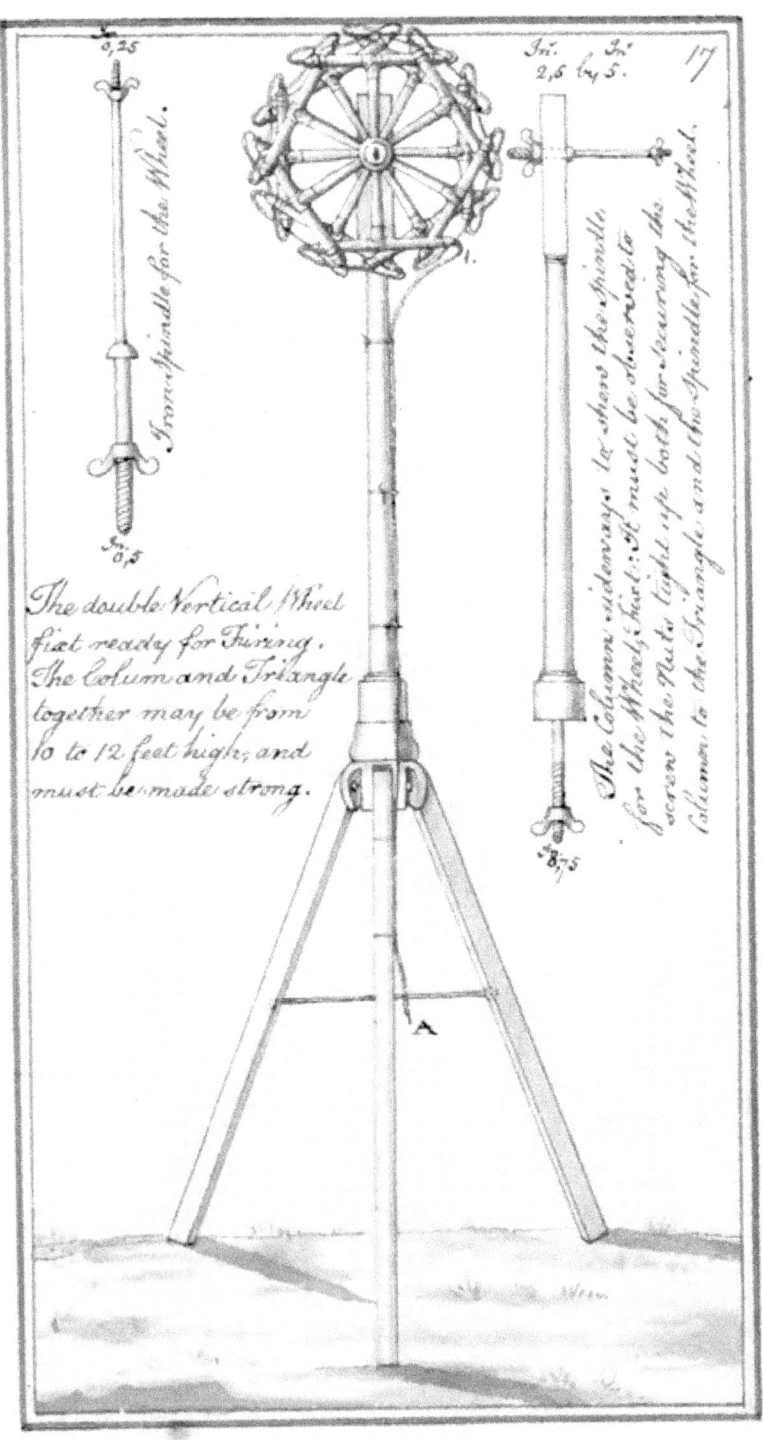

17
0,25
Iron Spindle for the Wheel.
In. 0,5
In. In.
2,5 by 5.
1.
The Column sideways to shew the Spindle for the Wheel, first: It must be observed to screw the Nuts tight up both for securing the Column to the Triangle and the Spindle for the Wheel.
8,75
The double Vertical Wheel fixt ready for Firing. The Colum and Triangle together may be from 10 to 12 feet high, and must be made strong.
A

Double Vertical Wheels for transparent Cyphers, Crowns, Coronets, Letters &c.

The Wheels for these are exactly the same as before, except that the method of leading them differs and which cannot well be Explained, further than that the leaders should not project beyond the ends of the Cases, for as the hole of the Box is just sufficient to let the Wheel work free, if either the ends of the leaders or the touches hang to the side of the Case from the bursting of the Communications, the motion of the Wheel will probably be stopt and spoil the intended Effect.

No Yellow Fire must be used for the interior Cases as it does not sufficiently illuminate; for the Outward six Cases two of them may be strong Yellow Fire and all the rest Brilliant.

Particular care is required in driving these Cases, for if one happens to Burst the Wheel is spoiled.

It will next be necessary to speak of the Boxes and Transparents.

The Boxes consists of a Circle of Fir

from

from two to six feet in diameter and from $\frac{5}{8}$ to $1\frac{1}{2}$ inch thick; these are [illegible] the Rock; exactly in the middle of the Circle must be an elm Block from an inch and a half to two inches thick and from 6 inches to 8 or [illegible] in diameter, screwed fast to the Back; the hole thro' the middle of the Block and Back may be from $\frac{3}{4}$ to 1 inch and $\frac{5}{8}$, and should be exactly centered for the Spindle to go freely through; round the Rim of the Back must be fixed a Circle of Ash hoop from $3\frac{1}{2}$ or 4 inches to six inches and a [illegible] of an inch thick; round the center Block is a Circle of fir from $\frac{1}{2}$ an inch to $\frac{3}{4}$ thick and about two or three inches broad; the inward Circle to be of such diameter as to give room for the Wheel to play round freely upon the Spindle.

The Boxes used in the Royal Laboratory are those of 4 and 6 feet; as smaller Boxes do not answer for the Works to be seen at a distance.

The following rough Sketches it is hoped

[illegible]

Front of the Box.

In.
4,0

4 Feet

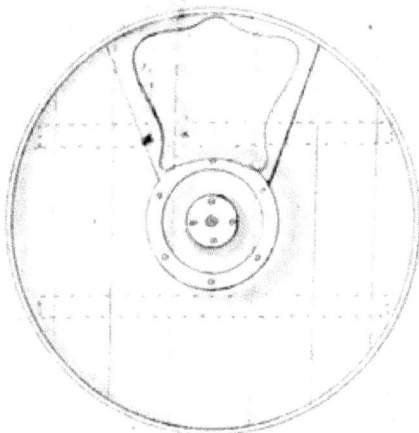

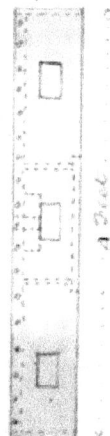

For a 2 Ounce Wheel.

6 Holes round the Hoop to let out the Smoke. 3 In. long by 1½ In. wide.

8 In.

2

In.
2,0 5

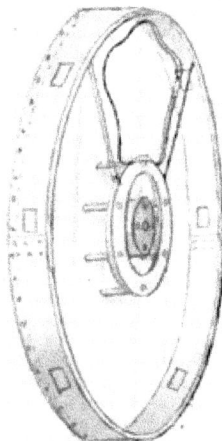

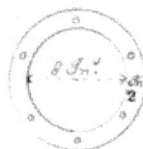

Small inward Circle – Fir and the 6 Pins Beech.

Center Block Elm.

[illegible] Boxes are made exactly in the [illegible] manner; only the dimensions [illegible] [illegible], all which must be regulated by the Wheel.

Now to shew the Method of Making the Transparents.

A Paste Board must be made of cartridge paper three thick and larger than the diameter of the Box an Inch or two; this being dry, find a Center and describe a Circle equal to the extreme diameter of the Box [illegible], with a [illegible] and black lead pencil, next describe both the interior and exterior diameters of the inward Circle, and if the interior circle or thickness of the Tin hoop is described it will be better.

Then the Paper must be cut off all round close to the exterior Circle, and the inward Circle of all taken quite out, so will the Paste board be made to fit the Box and its inward Circle.

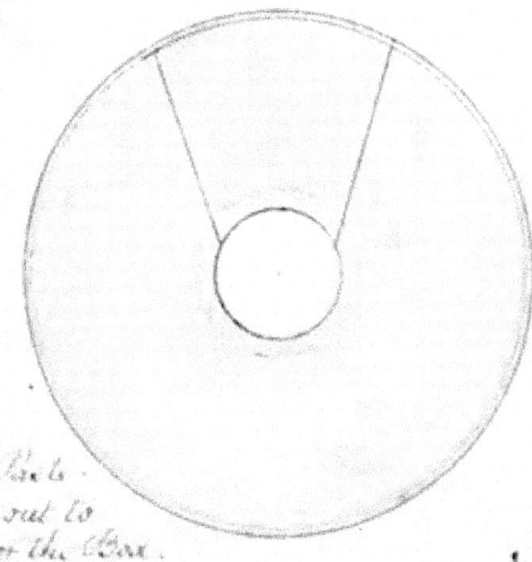

Circle of Paste board cut out to fit the Top of the Box.

Next to determine the Size of the Letters or other proper Device, it must be considered the inward Circle being 8 Inches, the half is = to 4 In.; the breadth of the inward Circle = 2 In. and the hoop ¼ In.: which is 6¼ In.s this subtracted from 2 feet leaves 1 Ft: 5 In. ¾ clear.
The Letters here are One foot in length.

It is hoped that these two Examples will be sufficient to elucidate the Method to be followed for any other Device.

The Letters are to be covered with yellow Persian Silk, laid on the back of the Pasteboard with paste and a small bristle brush; the Silk is not to be cut out to fit each Letter, but laid on first to try how many Letters it will cover at once, which is seldom above three, on account of being circular; always taking care to lay the right side of the Silk downwards and to cut it out to the best advantage.

There are two ways of Ordering the Crowns, Coronets &c.

First the Crown, Coronet &c. may be cut out in the pasteboard; and then the pasteboard must remain Circular.

The second Method, is to have the Crown, Coronet &c. cut out in Tin, so as to fit on the Ledgment or Frame at top joining to the Inward Circle, in this case, part of the pasteboard Circle must be cut away to the exterior of the Crown, Coronet &c. which is easily done by

laying

laying the tin Crown &c. on the paste-board, and marking it round with a black lead pencil.

After all is Silked, it should stand a day to dry; then the pasteboard and Crown may be nailed on to the Box with small Tacks; and the pasteboard before it is Silked should be done all over the Front side with size and whiting, if done after it is nailed on, care must be taken not to touch upon the Silk.

As it requires some judgment to cut out a Crown, Coronet &c. I beg leave to introduce an Example on a larger Scale.

Tin Crown.

By the foregoing Sketch it is visible that there must be a Margin left round each Compartment to paste the edges of the Silk on: the Yellow may be done with yellow Persian, but the Reds and Blues must be done with Crimson and Blue Sattin of about 6s p Yard; the large Beril at top must be done with white Persian or Sattin as likewise the Ermine below; the Beril must be tinted or coloured with verdigrease ground in oil, and the Ermine must have the shades and Spots done with black Colour in Oil, and likewise the Cap to be shaded with black.

The Method of Cutting out is by putting the Silk under the Crown, keeping the right side of the Silk upwards and with a black lead pencil mark it according to the outline of the Figure, then cut out the piece of Silk, and with a small brush lay on the paste all round the tin margin of the figure then lay on the piece of Silk pressing the edges close down all round, in like manner proceeding to Mark and Cut each piece one after

after another, pasting them on immediately, and where any two or more figures are alike, they may be cut out to one pattern. The Red for the Cap of the Crown is usually done last, after the rest is compleated.

Lastly to Fix the Box on the Column with it's triangle; first, the large Nut being taken off the iron at bottom of the Column, put it through the Block of the triangle; then the Column leaning on a trussel, the front leg of the triangle being lifted up, the large nut must be put on again and wrenched up tight, taking Care that the face of the Column fronts with the fore leg of the Triangle.

Next the large Nut must be taken off the Iron for the Wheel, and the end put through the Block of the Box and thro' the hole in the Column, then the large Nut to be screwed on again and the Center of the Crown being placed perpendicular with the middle line of the Column let the large Nut be wrenched up tight to the back of the Column so as to keep the Box quite steady.

Then

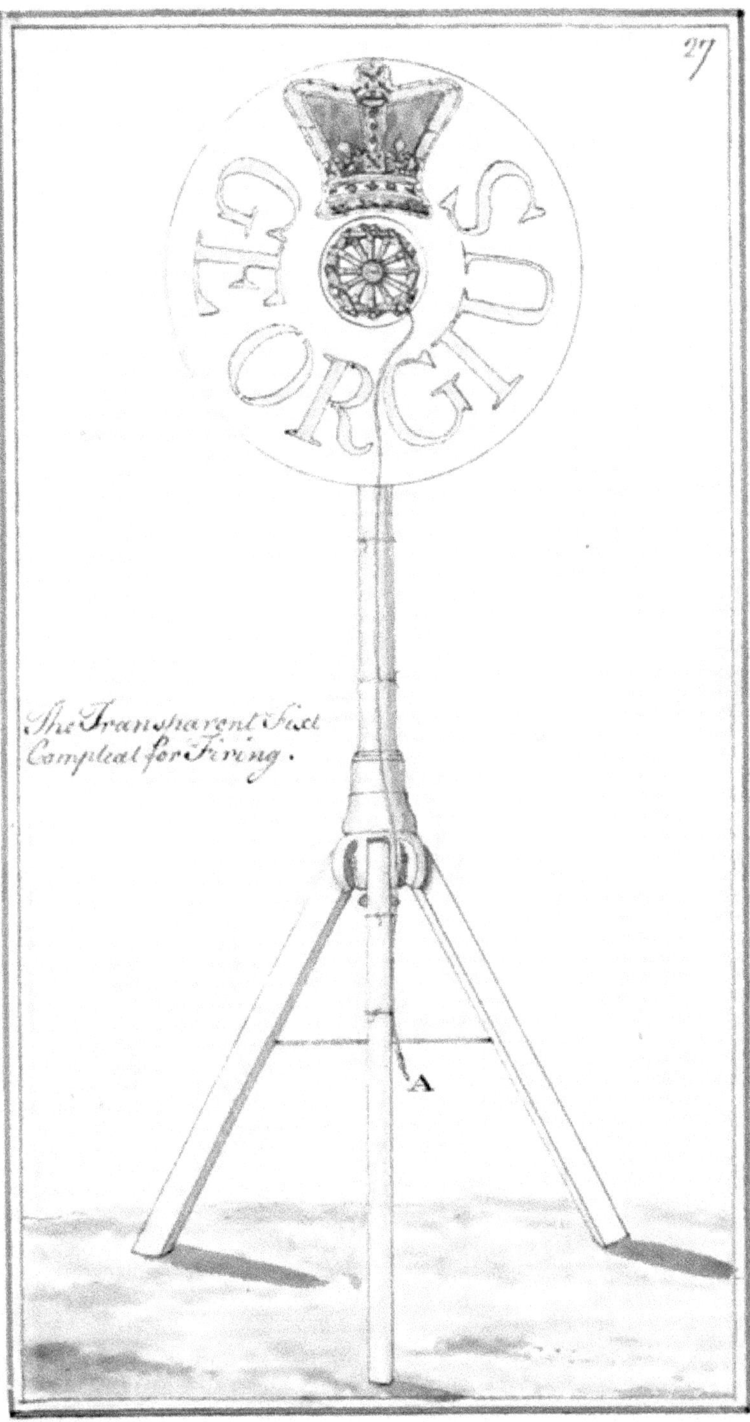
GEORGIUS
The Transparent Fixt
Compleat for Firing.
A

Then the small nut being taken off the Spindle, and the inside of the brass at each end of the Wheel oiled, put the Wheel upon the Spindle and try it works round free and easy; then screw on the small Nut and wrench it up tight but carefully so as not to strain the Spindle and let the Wheel be tried again to see that it runs free, without touching the Circle, then fix and tie the end of the long Communication into the Cartouch of the first Case in Front, and gently bending the leader bring it down to the Column securing it there in two or three Places with coarse twine or two easy turns of packthread, observing to let the leader have freedom, not to touch or lie upon the Front of the Box for fear it might damage the Silk.

Before the Piece is raised, with a soft brush or tool dipt in linseed oil,

gently

gently touch upon some places of all the sides of the Letters and Crown taking care not to go over upon the paper; the use of the Oil is to prevent the Line catching fire from the Sparks of the Brilliant.

Then let the Piece be raised up and set upon its legs, and being fronted to the proper point of View, set it perpendicular as the eye can judge, either by setting the front leg further out or in, and then gently tie the end of the long Communication to the front leg, which is done to prevent its being blown about by the wind and to keep it steady for Fireing.

It must be observed that the Cartouch on the first Case must be of varnished tube paper in order to resist rain &c and the lower end of the long Communication must have a slip of varnished paper put round to preserve the end of the Quickmatch from wet or accidental Sparks; this small slip must be taken off just

before

before the Piece is fired.

All the foregoing Precautions tho' long in Description, are short and easy in practice, and must be particularly attended to, if we wish to ensure Success.

Sometimes these Transparents are accompanied with a Sun or other Figure behind it and then if the Sun is separate from the Box, there needs no Alteration either to the Wheel or Box, but only to the Iron which must be long enough back from the Shoulder to go through the Box, through the Column and through the Block of the Sun and to screw behind.

The Cases for fixing the Sun with are called Sun Cases; these Cases are made of Cartoon paper, about 9 Inches long when finished and the diameter of the Bore 3/4 of an inch; the Method of making and Ordering Pasted Cartoon Cases of each Nature together with their application will be fully described in Page

These

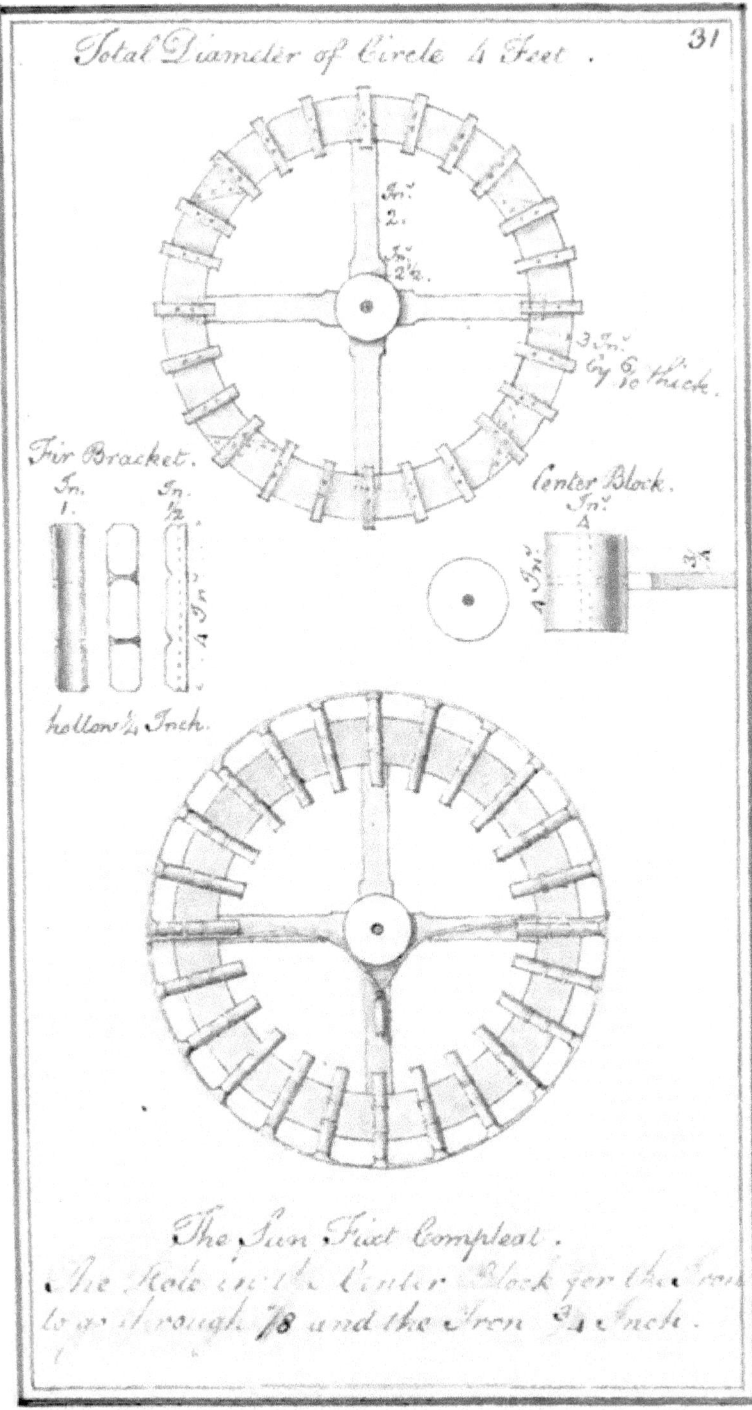

The Sun Fixt Compleat.

The Hole in the Center Block for the Iron to go through 7/8 and the Iron 3/4 Inch.

These Cases are generally drove with Brilliant Composition.

But first they must be prepared in the usual way, by stopping the vents with paper, then one ladlefull of Clay and 21 strokes with a 13 Inch Mallet, next two ladlefull of common fire with 21 strokes Ditto.

In the large way, it is necessary to have some hundreds of these Cases ready prepared; as it takes up some time.

Brilliant for Fan Cases.

	lb : oz : dr
Mealed Powder	1 : 2 : 0.
Salt Petre	0 : 4 : 8.
Sulphur	0 : 4 : 8.
Iron Filings	0 : 5 : 8.

To be Mixt in the usual manner.

One Ladlefull of Brilliant at a time and 21 strokes to each ladlefull with a 13 Inch Mallet, till the case is drove full enough to leave just room for one ladlefull of Clay at top.

It should be observed that these pasted Cases are not drove in Moulds, but cut in Brackets, one of which is secured tight in the grand Block and the Case fixed between the Brackets by means of a cord put tight round the notches of the Brackets, which are reversed to prevent the Brackets rising.

The following Sketch will illustrate this very plain

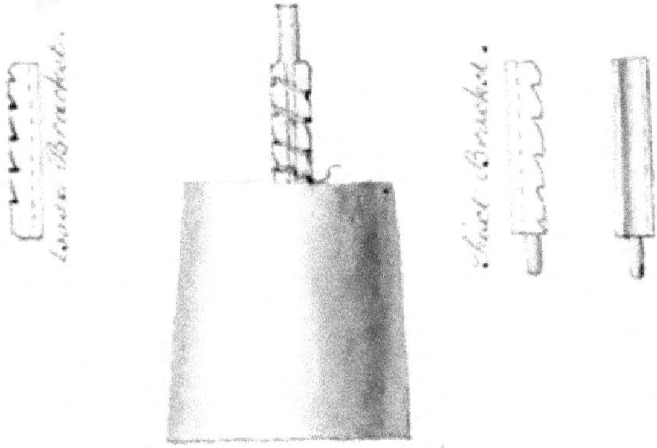

Loose Bracket.

Fixt Bracket.

Grand Block with the Case & Brackets fixt for Driving.

These Brackets must not be hollowed to meet quite close round the Case for then they cannot be fixt tight.

The Vent of these Cases is exactly 1/3 of the Bore and the Reamer must be particular to the Dimensions, taking care that it be not smaller, which would endanger the bursting of the Case.

The Reamer is in form like a gimblet only

only instead of a worm it has a nose like a common Bitt.

The choked end of each Case to be Bored just through the Clay to touch the common fire, then the top of the Common fire in each Case to be scratched a little with a round sharp pointed pricker; this is done to insure their taking fire; next they are to be primed with short piece of quick-match put in to fill the Vent and one piece stopt in tight with a round pointed pricker to secure the rest, then cut off the ends level with the top of the Case; Each Case to be primed with Quickmatch exactly in the same manner.

The other end of the Cases to be stopt full with pasted tube paper and all round about an inch over the end of the Case.

The Brackets round the Sun being strung with fine packthread begin at any Bracket and put in a Case placing it equally from each end of the Bracket, then draw the packthread tight and tie the Case firm; next it will be proper to have a Gauge made either of a piece of

leader

leader or a bit of stick cut and notched to the exact length that the quickmatch end of the Case stands from the end of the Bracket, by this Gauge all the Cases are to be set, in tying on to form the Circle and after the Cases are tied on, all the packthreads are to be covered over with pasted double tube paper about an inch broad, pressed close with the fingers.

To Lead or Communicate the Sun.

First each Case must have a length of coarse twine put round the Choke with a single tie at one side of the Case, letting the ends hang down four or five inches.

Then take a Cartridge paper leader and cut out out a piece a little longer than the diameter of a Case at top, apply the shoulder to the side of a Case and lay the leader along the ends of as many cases as it will reach marking or bending the leader exactly at the middle of each Case at top, and with the scissors cut out notches about half an inch in length at each bend or mark observing always to finish with a slip

at

at top of a case, then put a length of four thread Quickmatch thro' the leader and placing the shoulder of the first slip to the side of the first case measured from, produce the leader to the top of the next case so that the Quickmatch at the notch of the leader may touch the Quickmatch at top of the case, securing the leader at top of the case with the end of the middle finger of the left hand, then bring up the ends of twine — and with a single tie secure the leader at that side of the case, bring down the ends of twine and crossing them put them round the choke of the case; cross them again and bring up the ends of twine over the leader close to the side of the case at top, then tie down the leader at that side with a double knot, continuing to tie down the leader at the side of each case as far as the leader reaches, except the first and last ends, then cut off the ends of twine pretty near to the top of the leader.

Take another leader and cut a slip with

with a shoulder as at first, apply the slip over the top of the last case the end of the first leader reaches to, and mark as before by bending the leader a little at the quickmatch of each Case, and cut out notches exactly at the marks, then put a length of Quickmatch thro' the leader, observing to cut the end of the Quickmatch to a slope point at the first end of the second leader and put the sloped end of quickmatch into the last end of the first leader so that the ends of Quickmatch may join, bring down the joint to the top of the Case and tie it down on each side the case continuing to tie down the leader to each Case exactly as at first, observing to measure and join leader to leader and quickmatch to Quick-match all round.

The transverse Communication must be brought from the head of two opposite cases brought along the frames and secured with tacks, the two ends being laid down by the main Block and first tied together equally so that the ends of Quickmatch of one leader may touch the ends of the other

other, then a Cartouch of tube paper varnished must be put on the ends of the two leaders and tied on with coarse twine, after which a nail is to be drawn in (between the twine which lies on the Cartouch and in the middle between the two leaders) to keep the Cartouch steady.

Lastly the whole to be pasted with double tube paper, over the end of each Case and a piece put all round each case and all the leaders particularly all over the cross communication and round part of the Cartouch, above it and on each side of it securing it well from accidents by Rain or fire; then set it to dry; and when dry, let it be Varnished all over the pasted parts.

When the Sun is fixed behind the Column as before remarked, a long leader or Communication must be fixed or tied in the Cartouch then tied behind the Column in two or three places; and when the Piece and Stand are raised upright and set in the proper place, the end of this last Communication must be tied to

one

one of the off legs of the Triangle, as it ought by no means to interfere with the communication belonging to the Wheel least one should fire the other: but as soon as the Wheel finishes, fire must be given to the Sun.

There is a superior Method of Managing Suns or other Figures behind the Transparent Boxes, by which, the fire is immediately conveyed to them as soon as the last Case of the Wheel finishes; this will be particularly explained in higher Order of Communications.

Former for Rolling the Cartouches.

Cartouch.

The Cartouches are made of Tube paper, consisting of four or five turns in thickness, and 3 inches long; they are of different sizes, some to contain the end of one leader, some two; some three and some four; it is easy to determine the size by the leaders: the method of Rolling them is very easy after the Paper is cut out, they are to be

rolled

rolled one at a time putting a little paste on the outward edge, then put in trays to dry and when thoroughly dry to be Varnished; One Man will roll a thousand of these in a day.

Rough Sketch of the Sun with the Cases tied on and strung with twine; one leader tied on, the second ready.

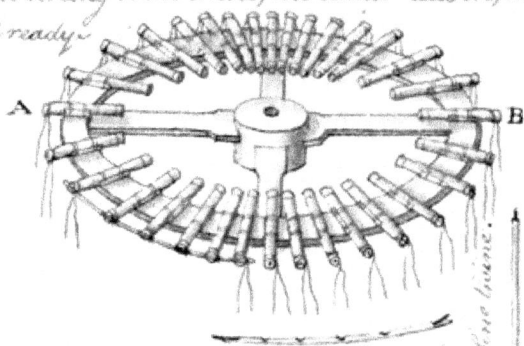

After the Sun has been led all round; the Cross Communication must be fixt to any two opposite Cases as at A & B, and secured with tacks.

The Cross Communication Quickmatched & tied together.

The Cross Communication as before with its Cartouch.

each end about an inch over the other tied in two places; then push the small end of the leader & match up into the mouth; choke and tie them.

Method of Making the Long Communications; Each Leader having a trumpet Mouth, a length of Match run through and the two ends tied with fine twine.

Long Communication Compleat, to be fixed in the Cartouch of the Cross Communication just before the Piece is raised up.

Sky Rockets.

There are several Natures of them; but only 2 Pounder Signal Rockets are applied to Military purposes.

The Moulds are made of Brass in the Laboratory, but Wood Moulds made of Box or Lignum Vitæ answer very well

Rockets in general use, are Quarter Pounders, Half Pounders and One Pounders for Fireworks, and these are always headed with Stars or Rains; Quarter Pound Rockets are used only for Flights and are either Bounced or Capped with Stars.

Rockets are drove solid in the Laboratory and afterwards Bored in a Lathe; but there is a Method of driving them hollow by means of an iron spindle fixt upright in the Mould and then the drifts must be hollow so as to go freely over the Spindle, this last Method requires great care and is too dangerous, unless for those expert at driving.

The Cases for all Rockets are to be Rolled dry, that is, without any paste; and therefore this

this Work is generally done in the Winter.

TABLE of the Dimensions of Rocket Moulds.

Body of the Mould.

Length of the Body.	Diam.r of the Bore.													
ab.	de.													
diam.n	In: 10s													
F. 7.	6,25													
7.	4,60													
7.	4,10													
7.	3,10													
7.	2,70													
7.	2,15													
7.	1,70													
7.	1,35													
7.	1,70													

The first Method of this Table would have been too intricate, therefore judged it better to Refer all the Moulds to the annexed Draught and Scale.

As the Diameter of the Bore of each Mould is given in the above Table, it will be easy to raise a Scale of Calibres; and by Measuring the proportional parts on this Draught and Scale, the Dimensions of the other Moulds may be laid down.

The 14: 20 & 50 Pounders have no Moulds.

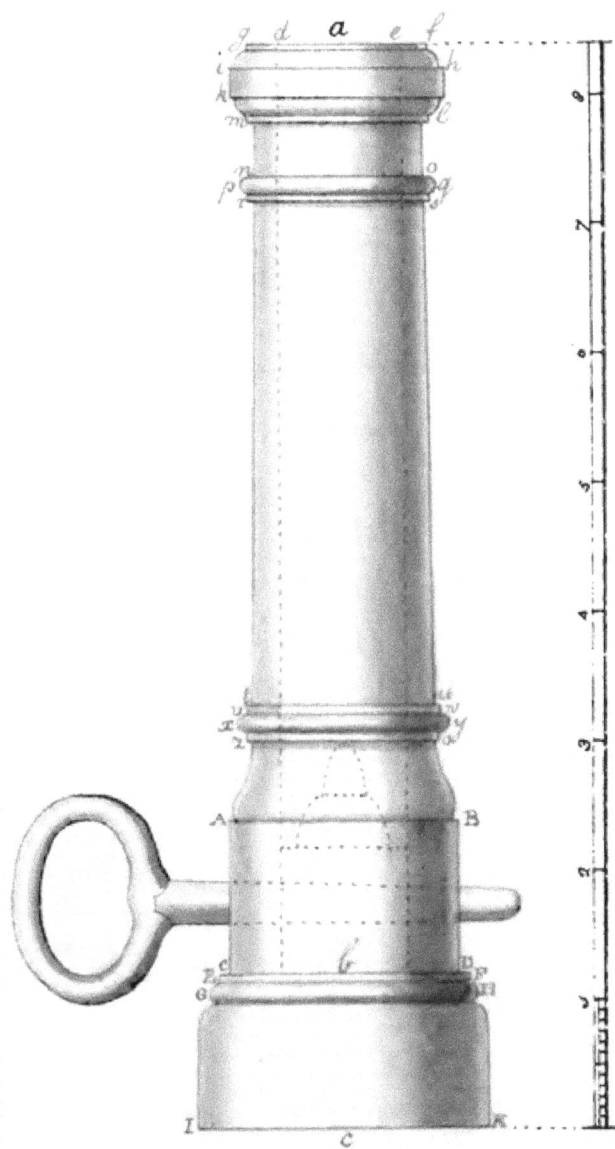

A Scale of Diameters, each Diameter equal to the Bore of the Mould.

Sky Rocket Mould.

44

The Case to be 7½ diameters in length when compleated; But the paper must be Cut equal to 9⁶ Diameters to Allow for the Choke & Cutting at each end.

Scale of Callibers.

The Rocket Case Compleatly Rolled and Marked.

4½
4
3½
3

¾ of ⅙

2½

1 2 3 4 5 6

Rule for finding the Vent of all Sky Rockets, Divide the Bore diametrically into 6 equal parts; The Vent shall be 2½ sixth parts and the top of the Bore ¾ of a sixth part.

To Roll the Rocket Cases.

First the Paper must be cut out suitable to the Nature of Cases to be Rolled; a whole Quire at a time marking out the paper according to the Pattern, the principal part is the Slope which must be always equal to the exterior Circumference of a Case; which may be easily calculated from the given diameters, either by the common or Matius proportion of the diameter to the Circumference.

The exterior Diameter of a ¼ Pd. Case is In. 1,06.

```
7 ....22 ...106
             22
           ----
            212
           212      In.
       7)2332(3,33
           23
            22
             2
```

By the Proportion gives In. 3,33 for the breadth of the Slope, but the Pattern has 3½ Inches which is a little more and makes the spiral

sit

sit closer so that the best way is to regulate the Slope by the diameter of the Bore of the Mould.

The other Articles necessary for Rolling, are, Wood Formers; Wood Nipples; Wood Gauges; Cutters of Wood; Rolling Boards; Sharp knives; fine or coarse packthread or Line for tying down the Chokes; Hamburgh Line to rig the Choking Engine and Mallets.

Dimensions of Cases and Formers for Rockets.

Nature of Rockets.	The Case.				The Former.			
	Exter.r Diam.r of Case.	Inter.r Diam.r of Case.	Thickness of Case.	Length of Empty Case.	Diam.r of Body.	Length of Body.	Diam.r of Handle.	Length of Handle.
	In.s: 10	In.s: 10	In.s 10	Ft. In.: 10	In.s: 10	Ft. In.: 10	In.s: 10	In.s: 10
50 Po.d	6,23	4,475	0,8757	3:10,735	4,475	4:6,000	6,23	8,0
20	4,59	3,298	0,6459	2:10,425	3,298	3:6,000	4,59	8,0
14	4,07	2,923	0,5233	2:6,525	2,923	3:0,000	4,07	6,0
6	3,07	2,205	0,4321	1:11,026	2,205	2:3,000	3,07	6,0
4	2,68	1,926	0,3768	1:8,100	1,926	2:0,000	2,68	5,0
2	2,13	1,529	0,3002	1:3,975	1,529	1:6,000	2,13	5,0
1	1,69	1,214	0,2378	1:0,675	1,214	1:2,000	1,69	4,0
½	1,34	0,961	0,1893	0:10,050	0,961	1:0,000	1,34	3,5
¼	1,06	0,761	0,1493	0:8,250	0,761	0:10,000	1,06	3,0

Dimensions of Wood Nipples, Gauge's & Cutters.

	The Wood Nipple.			Wood Gauges.			Wood Cutters.		
	Length of Nipple ab	Diam. of Nipple da	Length of the Part ac	Length of Choking ab	Length for the Case cd	Total Length ef	Diameter at each End	Diameter at the Middle.	Total Length.
	In.s 10	In.s: 10	In.s: 10	In.s: 10	In.s: 10	In.s: 10	In.s: 10	In.s: 10	Ft. In.: 10
50	3,12	1,665	3,12	4,5	Half a Calliber	From 3 to 6 Inch.s	4,300	5,000	From 3 to 8 In.s
20	2,30	1,372	2,30	3,5			3,000	3,500	
14	2,03	1,217	2,03	3,0			2,700	3,250	
6	1,53	0,917	1,53	2,5			2,000	2,500	
4	1,34	0,802	1,34	2,125			1,700	2,200	
2	1,60	0,637	1,60	1,5			1,400	1,800	
1	0,85	0,505	0,85	1,25			1,000	1,500	
½	0,67	0,400	0,67	1,0			0,800	1,200	
¼	0,53	0,317	0,53	0,75			0,600	1,000	

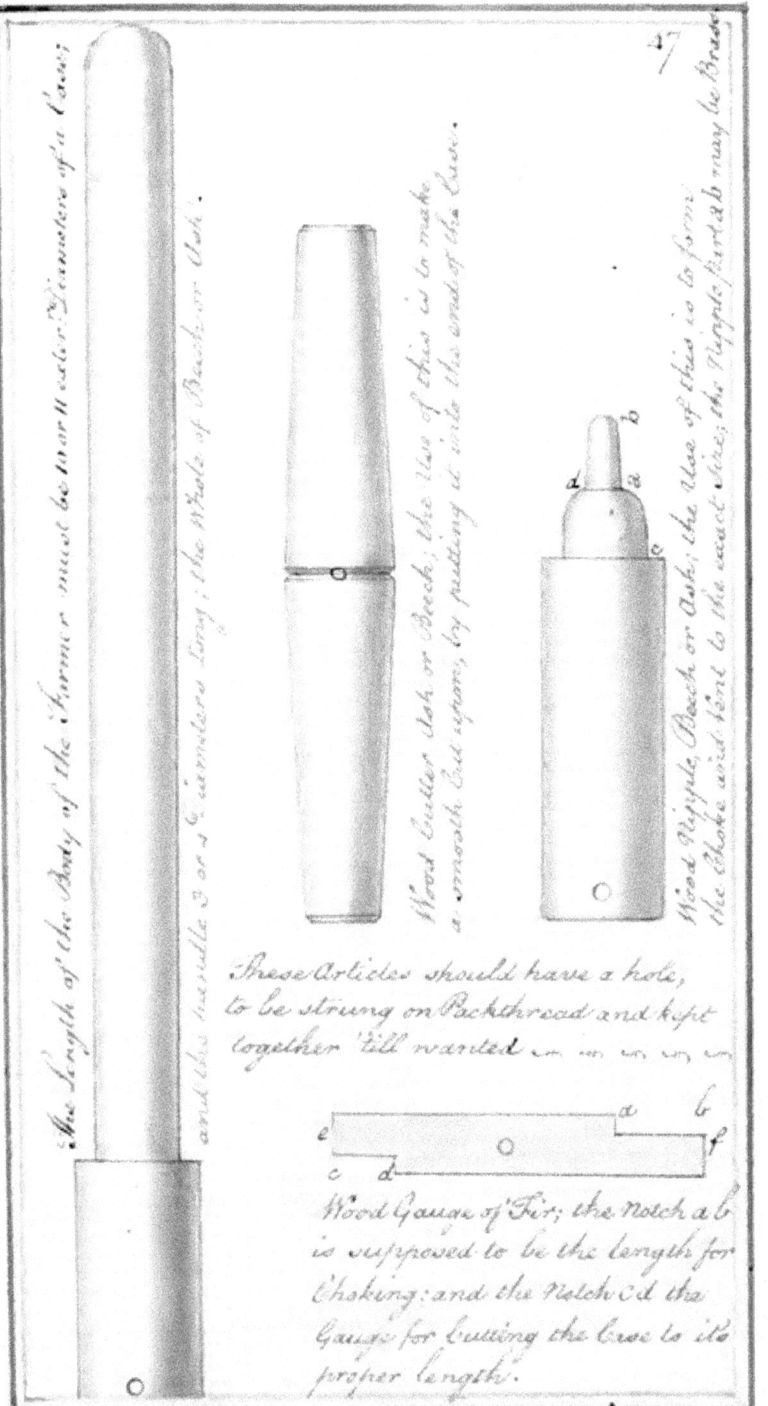
47
The Length of the Body of the Former must be 10 or 11 exter: Diameters of a Case;
and the handle 3 or 4 Diameters long; the Whole of Beech or Ash.
Wood Cutter Ash or Beech; the Use of this is to make
a smooth Cut upon, by putting it into the end of the Case.
d
b
a
c
Wood Nipple, Beech or Ash; the Use of this is to form
the Choke and bent to the exact Size; the Nipple part a b may be Brass
These Articles should have a hole,
to be strung on Packthread and kept
together 'till wanted
e
a
b
f
c
d
Wood Gauge of Fir; the Notch a b
is supposed to be the length for
Choking: and the Notch c d the
Gauge for Cutting the Case to it's
proper length.

Method of Rolling the Cases; The paper being laid on the Table and the Wood Former upon the Paper, the end a b must be brought over the Former upon the paper beneath, then creased close to the Body of the Former with the fingers all along, then turned quick over and Rolled up tight, then it must have five or six turns under the Rolling-board and be tried in the Mould to see if it Fits, if the Case is too low or small for the Mould, part of the paper must be unrolled and a Slip put in then Rolled up again and three or four turns given with the Rolling Board then tried again; if still too low, unroll and put in another slip proceeding as before till the Case is brought to fit the Mould.

If again the Case is too high to go into the Mould, unroll and cut off a slip still observing the same slope as at first, Roll up again and try, if still too high, cut off another slip, continuing till it fits the Mould.

By Fitting the Mould, is to be under-stood,

Sketch 1st

Rolling Board.

a

b

-stood, that it must go into the Mould so as just to be pusht through without too much straining, neither too tight nor too slack.

Care should be taken, where Slips are necessary, to put them in so as not to make the Case thicker of Paper in one part than another.

The Case being brought to fit, push it so far through as to leave just sufficient to make a smooth end, then draw back the Former to make room to put in the Cutter of wood tight, and with a sharp knife cut all round by the end of the Mould close home to the Cutter to make a smooth end, then take out the Cutter and take off the superfluous paper; there must be a Cutting Board to lay the Mould on, for it would

spoil

spoil the Table to cut upon it.

Sketch 2^d.

a

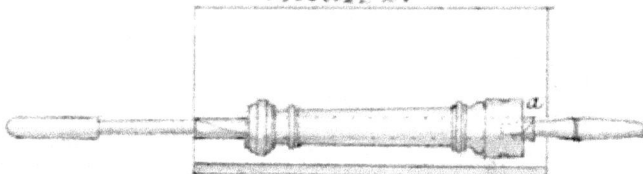

The Former, Case, Mould and Cutter of Wood fixed in order to cut off the rough end of Paper close by the end of the Mould at a.

To Choke the Case, push it through about an inch and apply the fir Gauge for the Choke to it, and set the end of the Case exactly to the Gauge,

Sketch 3^d.

Gauge for Choke.

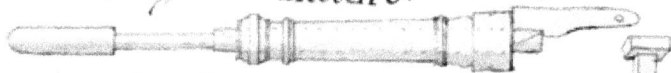

as in this Sketch.

Then take it to the Choking Engine and put the Cord round the Case close to the end of the Mould, next put the nipple into the end of the Case as in this Sketch; holding the Mould in the left hand, the left foot on the Block and the right foot on the end of the

Sketch 4th.

A

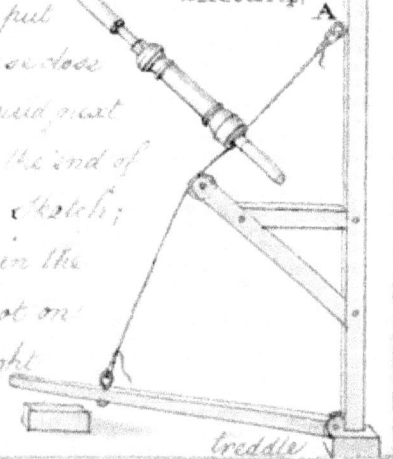

treddle

treddle, holding the end or handle of the Nipple with the right hand, press steadily on the treddle till the case is creased all round, then press harder on the treddle turning the Mould with the left hand upwards towards A, this turning the Mould round a little at a time is to be done between every rest with the foot in treading, then work it downwards again by degrees towards the Pully, now and then easing off the line and setting it on afresh till the case is Choked close to the Nipple all round, when the Nipple must be taken out and the Choking line being eased off, with all expedition proceed to tie down the Choke.

Sketch 5th

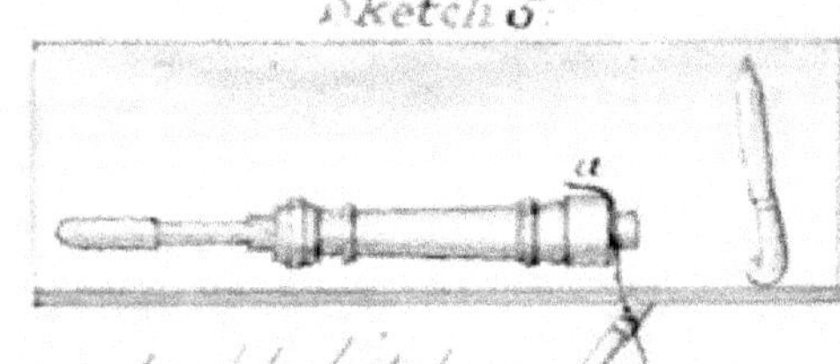

First give a double hitch round the Choke, and placing the left thumb on the end of the packthread at a, take the wood Cutter in the right hand take three or four turns of packthread round it and placing the end under the table

table strain the hitches tight, then ease of the Cutter, and make another hitch straining it tight as before, and so on for six or seven hitches one after another as quick as they can be done, always straining each hitch tight, then cut off the ends of packthread at about a ¼ of an inch from the Choke.

Quarter Pound, Half Pound, 1 Pound and 2 Pound Rockets are all to be Choked in this one Method, only the larger the Rocket the more time and Care is required. For tying the Chokes of ¼ Pound Rockets fine packthread is used; For ½ Pound Cases Middling packthread; For 1 Pounder One Pounder Quilting line; and for 2 Pounders 1½ Pounder Quilting line.

The next Article is to set down the Choke and for this purpose it is necessary to have what is called a Setter, this is made in all respects like the Former, only the Body of the Setter is a small matter less in diameter so as to go easier into the Case; the foot of the Mould must likewise be be plain, having a Wart but no Nipple; then to proceed, take the former out of the Case and put in the Setter, place the Body of the Mould with Case and Setter on the plain foot and give five or six strokes with a Mallet on the head of the Setter to set down the Choke. —

Sketch of the Plain Foot of the Mould for Setting down the Chokes of Cases on; These Bottoms should be Marked the same as the Mould.

Having set down the Choke, take off the Body of the Mould with the Case and Setter and placing the Mould on the Cutting Board, take out the Setter; next the Choke end of the Case must be set by the Gauge equal to half a Calliber or diameter and the wood Cutter being put tight into the other end of the Case with a sharp knife cut off the superfluous paper at that end close and even with the end of the Mould, take out the Cutter and pull off the

the Cutting, then push the Case out of the Mould and lay it by; proceeding to Roll and Compleat each Case exactly in the same manner, and to cut all cases of one nature exactly of equal Length.

All Rocket Cases for Heading, when compleated to be 7½ Callibers from end to end; for as the Body of the Mould is 7 Callibers long, the Case must be longer that there may be some purchase to pull the Rocket out by when drove.

Half Pounder, One and Two Pounder Cases require from two to four lengths of paper to Compleat the thickness; the Method of Rolling is first to Roll up one piece within three or four inches then lay the end of the second piece over the end of the first, continue to Roll up as before placing one piece in after the other, the last piece only must have the proper Slope; the principal points are to place the second paper so far over the end of the first as to make a whole turn and to lay each paper straight so as to Roll up even at the ends with the first.

A sufficient Number of Cases being Rolled, they must be marked at 3½ and 4½ Diameters and at the Clay which is always ⅓ of a diameter, each Case should likewise have the N.o or mark of the Mould they were Rolled in and the Rollers Name and time when Rolled; these Marks are commonly measured with a pair of Compasses, but a Gauge may be made of stiff paper to answer the purpose.

The Cases to be made up in parcels of half a dozen in each and packt up in a dry Store room 'till wanted.

Four and six pounder Cases are Rolled in Moulds and may be choked in a Choking Engine, but the larger Rockets are to be Choked by means of a strong Pole put into a Beam at bottom of the Wall, to a Beam in the Cieling is a strong staple fixed having a double length of Cord equally spliced, to these and to a Ring in the pole the Choking Line is to be fixed; this being pressed upon by two or three men

forces

forces the Choke close, but the same managements must be used as in the Choking Engine and the large Cases will require two Men to handle and work them.

Driving of Rockets.

Composition.

	lb: oz.
Salt Petre	4: 0.
Sulphur	1: 0.
Charcole	1: 8.

To Mix the Composition; the Salt Petre and Charcole to be put together on a mixing table and well rubbed together with the hands for about ten minutes or a quarter of an hour, then add the Sulphur to it and mix all well together with the hands, then sifted through a fine hair Sieve four times, then rubbed between the hands again and sifted four times through the hair Sieve.

The use of rubbing the Ingredients

together

together is to prevent the Charcole from flying about which would make it bad Sifting besides losing part of the Charcole.

The Composition to be put into a leather Bottom covered with a sheep skin and kept in a separate Room; to be fetcht in the square fir Boxes as wanted.

Articles necessary for Driving.

Rocket Cases and Moulds; Strong Elm Blocks with a hole to set the foot of the Mould in; Wood Drifts; Wood Mallets; Copper Ladles; wood scrapers; a small piece of round cane; and clay in a square fir Box.

The foot of the Mould having a Nipple to it must be used for Driving and the Key set tight; the Block for the Mould to stand on must be of a convenient height so that a person may sit and drive with ease.

The first or longest Drift must be

hollowed

hollowed at the end so as to go freely over the Nipple on the foot of the Mould, this Drift is used for setting down the Case in the Mould and for driving the Composition 'till No. 2 will reach to drive with; as soon as the Mark on No. 2 is exactly even with the top of the Case proceed to use No. 3 'till its mark comes even with the top of the case; then No. 4 must be used 'till the mark a is even with the top of the Case which is the whole height of Composition to be drove; then put in a ladlefull of Clay which must be drove down 'till the three dots on the drift are exactly even with the top of the Case, giving the same number of strokes to the Clay as to a ladlefull of Composition.

It will be necessary to observe particularly on the copper Ladles, which must be curiously adapted to each Nature of Rockets, for unless these are exact the driving will be imperfect, that is, so many

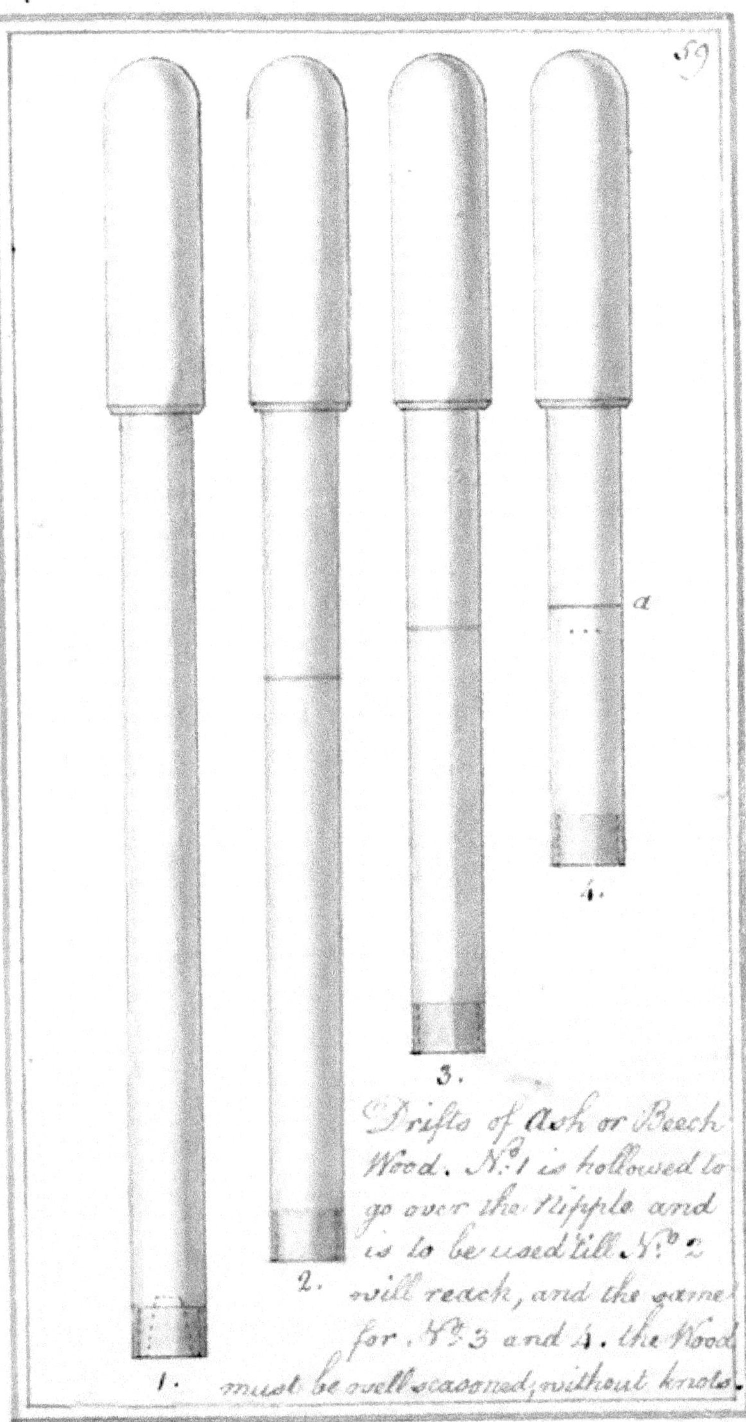
a
1.
2.
3.
4.
Drifts of Ash or Beech Wood. N.o 1 is hollowed to go over the Nipple and is to be used till N.o 2 will reach, and the same for N.o 3 and 4. the Wood must be well seasoned; without knots.

many ladlesfull of Composition when drove down should exactly fill up to 4½ diameters.

TABLE of the Dimensions of Copper Ladles for Sky Rockets of each Nature.

Nature	The Ladle Pattern							The Handle			
	Lengths.				Diameters.						Total Length
	ab	ac	dc	cb	ef	gh	ik	ab	cd	ac	
Pounds	In: 10	In: 10	In: 10	In: 10	In: 10	In: 10	In: 10	In: 10	In: 10	In: 10	In: 10
50..	12,09	9,34	1,7	2,75	8,59	13,9	14,0	4,30	4,375	2,75	9,0
20..	8,88	6,80	1,25	2,00	6,33	9,9	10,0	3,125	3,198	2,00	8,0
14..	7,85	6,10	1,10	1,75	5,82	8,7	8,8	2,775	2,823	1,75	7,0
.6..	5,90	4,60	0,83	1,30	4,20	6,65	6,7	2,055	2,105	1,30	5,0
.4..	5,17	4,02	0,75	1,15	3,70	5,75	5,8	1,776	1,826	1,15	5,0
.2..	4,00	3,19	0,58	0,90	2,935	4,58	4,6	1,429	1,479	0,90	4,0
.1..	3,33	2,53	0,45	0,80	2,33	3,63	3,65	1,115	1,164	0,80	4,0
.½..	2,71	2,01	0,36	0,75	1,84	2,87	2,88	0,900	0,95	0,70	3,6
.¼..	2,24	1,50	0,3	0,65	1,50	2,25	2,3	0,700	0,75	0,65	3,6

N:B. The length of the Bowl or Belly of each ladle from a to c is equal to 1½ diam;ʳ of the exterior diameter of a Rocket and the other parts in proportion; the Curve ge, fh, must be found on the line giorhk being only an inverted Ovolo.

The

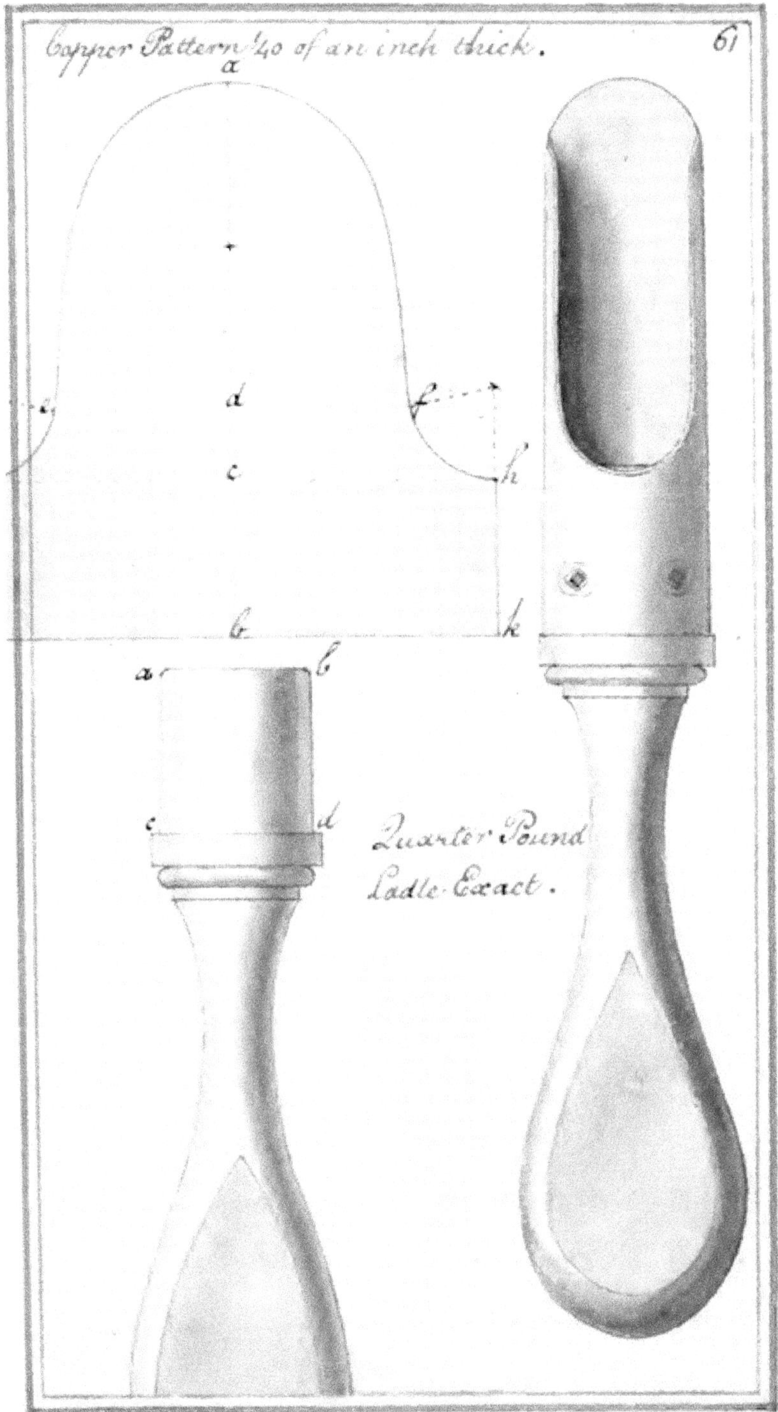
Copper Pattern 1/40 of an inch thick.
a
d
c
e
f
h
b
k
a
b
c
d
Quarter Pound
Ladle Exact.

The Drifts for each Nature of Rockets may be very easily ordered as follows, according to the foregoing Sketches; the long or hollow drift serves to drive 3/4 of a diameter, and the other three 1/4 Diameter each; and there should be a short drift the same as No. 4 for driving the Clay only, because the Clay sticks to the end of the drift and requires to be scraped off every time the drift is used.

In using the long hollow drift, great care must be taken to clear all the composition from the hollow by striking on the head of the drift with the Mallet till it is clear, holding the drift in the left hand over the Composition Box; and this must be done every time after driving a ladlefull of Composition with it; otherwise there will be danger, either of splitting the drift or exciting fire.

Let all the drifts go free and easy into the

the case so as not to bind or be stiff nor too low or slack, but only just to have play, for it is very troublesome driving when the drifts go too tight.

In driving, the handle of the Drift should be held lightly between the thumb and forefinger of the left hand, with which the drift is to be kept playing round and lifted up a little between each stroke, by this method the Composition is drove more solid than when the drift is kept without motion as some do.

Filling the Ladle, consists in dipping it into the Composition taking up as much as it can; then the Small round bit of Cane must be passed equally along the top of the ladle to take off the superfluous Composition, that the ladle may be exactly full to the edges; this must be observed at every ladlefull, and is called striking the Ladle.

In Using the Mallet, it should not be held too stiff, the motion should be free and the strokes as equal as possible taking care to count the exact number to each

each ladlefull of Composition, giving neither more nor less.

A Two Pounder Rocket, to each ladlefull 31 Strokes with a pound Rocket Mallet Wt: lb: oz 3:8.

A 1 Pounder Rocket, to each ladlefull 21 Strokes with a pound Rocket Mallet Wt: lb: oz 3:8.

A 1/2 Pound Rocket, to each ladlefull 18 Strokes with a 13 Inch Mallet Wt: lb: oz 2:1.

A 1/4 Pound Rocket, to each ladlefull 15 Strokes with a 10 Inch Mallet Wt: lb: oz 1:10.

Four and Six pound Rockets may be drove with a two handed Mall of Lignum Vitæ Wt: lb: oz 7:8, this requires two persons, one to hold the drift and feed the case, and the other to drive with the Mall; the number of Strokes to each ladlefull for a 4 Pounder 31 and the 6 Pounder 41.

there is a small Engine for driving 4 and 6 Pound Rockets and then the No of strokes to each ladlefull is 21 & 31.

14, 20 and 50 Pound Rockets are to be drove in the Engine, of which there were three

three Natures formerly fixt in Nº 10. these Engines are in the nature of Pile Engines, except that these are worked with a rope and a large Wheel at top, much like ringing a Bell, the Blocks are of lignum vitæ, and the Moulds for holding the Cases are of oak in two parts well secured together with strong screw bolts and Nuts; there is no account of the Nº of strokes to each ladlefull for each; but it will be easy to regulate this by comparing the square of the diameter of Composition, the Weight of the Mallet and force for a 2 Pounder, with the 3 last mentioned, in proportion.

TABLE of the Work.

Nature of Rockets.	One Man can Roll in one day.	Nº one Man drives in one day.	Nº One Man Bores in one day.	Nº One Man Reams in one day.	Nº One Man Heads in one day.
2 Poun.ds	18	18	60	24	24
1	24	24	60	24	24
1/2	36	36	80	36	36
1/4	60	60	120	60	60

The

The next Article after driving, is to Bore the Rockets, this in the Laboratory is performed in a Lathe and requires two persons, one to turn the Wheel and the other to fix and attend the Rockets.

The Boxes and Bitts are the principal articles and should be very exact; there are four Boxes, vizt. one for two Pounders, Ditto for One Pounders; Ditto for ½ Pounders, and one for ¼ Pounders; the Boxes are made exactly to fit into each other, and the interior is equal to the exterior diam^r. of the Rocket they are to receive, so as the Rocket may fit in rather tight; the length of each Box is made several inches longer than the case for the convenience of wedging the Rocket tight at the open end, and on account of the Boxes fitting.

At the head of each Box is a square brass plate fixt flush with screws; in the center of the Plate is a hole for the Bitt just to go through so as to clear out with the Composition, the Brass plate is only at the head of the principal Box which

which contain the others, and of which there are two Setts, Viz.t

1.st One large sliding Box for 14 Pound Rockets, containing a Box for 6 Pounders, which contains a Box for two Pounders and a Box for 1/2 Pounders which fits into the two Pounder Box.

2.d A large Sliding Box, containing a Box for 1/4 Pound Rockets which contains a Box for 1 Pounders and a Box for 1/4 Pou.rs which fits into the 1 Pounder Box.

All the Boxes are made of Oak and each Large sliding Box is furnished with two brass ledges 1/10 of an inch thick set on firm and flush with brass screws; the other Boxes fit close into each other that the Rockets may be kept steady as possible; the Bottom of each Box close to the head has an Oblong hole cut through that the Composition which comes out of the Rockets in Boreing may fall into a Box set underneath and which likewise receives the Clearings from the Bill.

The following Tables and Sketches are the exact

TABLE of the Dimensions of Boxes for Fixing Sky Rockets of each Nature in for Boreing them in the Lathe. Royal Laboratory.

Nature of Boxes for each Sett.	Exterior Sliding Boxes. Head of the Sliding Box.										Back of Sliding Box					Interr. Boxes which fit into each other. Head of Interr. Boxes.							Back of Intr. Boxes				
	ab	ac	eg	gh	ik	kl	mn	mo	ip	pk	ab	fg	cd	ce	hi	ab	ac	ef	ce	fi	gh	g	ab	fg	cd	ce	hi
Boxes	I.,10	I.,10	I.,10	I.,10	I.,10	I.,10	I.,10	I.,10	I.,10	I.,10	I.,10	I.,10	I.,10	I.,10	I.,10	I.,10	I.,10	I.,10	I.,10	I.,10	I.,10	I.,10	I.,10	I.,10	I.,10	I.,10	I.,10
1st Sett. 14 Pr.	6,83	2,8	2,0	5,3	4,08	1,01	2,0	0,9	4,0	5,0	2,9	1,0	2,5	1,3	1,0	...	...	...	...	...	...	...	...	...	...	...	...
.6	...	...	...	...	...	...	...	...	...	...	...	...	...	...	...	4,07	3,9	3,07	0,49	0,5	1,46	0,1	2,8	0,5	1,9	1,2	0,96
.2	...	...	...	...	...	...	...	...	...	...	...	...	...	...	...	3,0	3,46	2,09	0,48	0,48	1,04	0,36	2,33	0,5	1,4	1,3	0,95
.½	...	...	...	...	...	...	...	...	...	...	...	...	...	...	...	2,02	2,95	1,32	0,35	0,41	0,67	0,23	2,1	0,42	1,0	1,3	0,96
2d. Sett. 12 Pr.	6,8	3,0	1,8	5,3	3,8	0,95	2,0	0,7	4,0	5,0	2,6	1,0	3,7	1,65	1,0	...	...	...	...	...	...	...	...	...	...	...	...
.4	...	...	...	...	...	...	...	...	...	...	...	...	...	...	...	3,78	3,95	2,7	0,55	0,55	1,1	0,4	2,48	0,55	3,25	1,65	1,0
.1	...	...	...	...	...	...	...	...	...	...	...	...	...	...	...	2,67	3,12	1,67	0,52	0,52	0,82	0,35	2,32	1,0	2,3	1,65	1,0
.½	...	...	...	...	...	...	...	...	...	...	...	...	...	...	...	1,6	2,95	1,0	0,3	0,3	0,47	0,35	1,0	0,7	1,3	1,0	1,0

exact proportions for each Sett of Boxes.

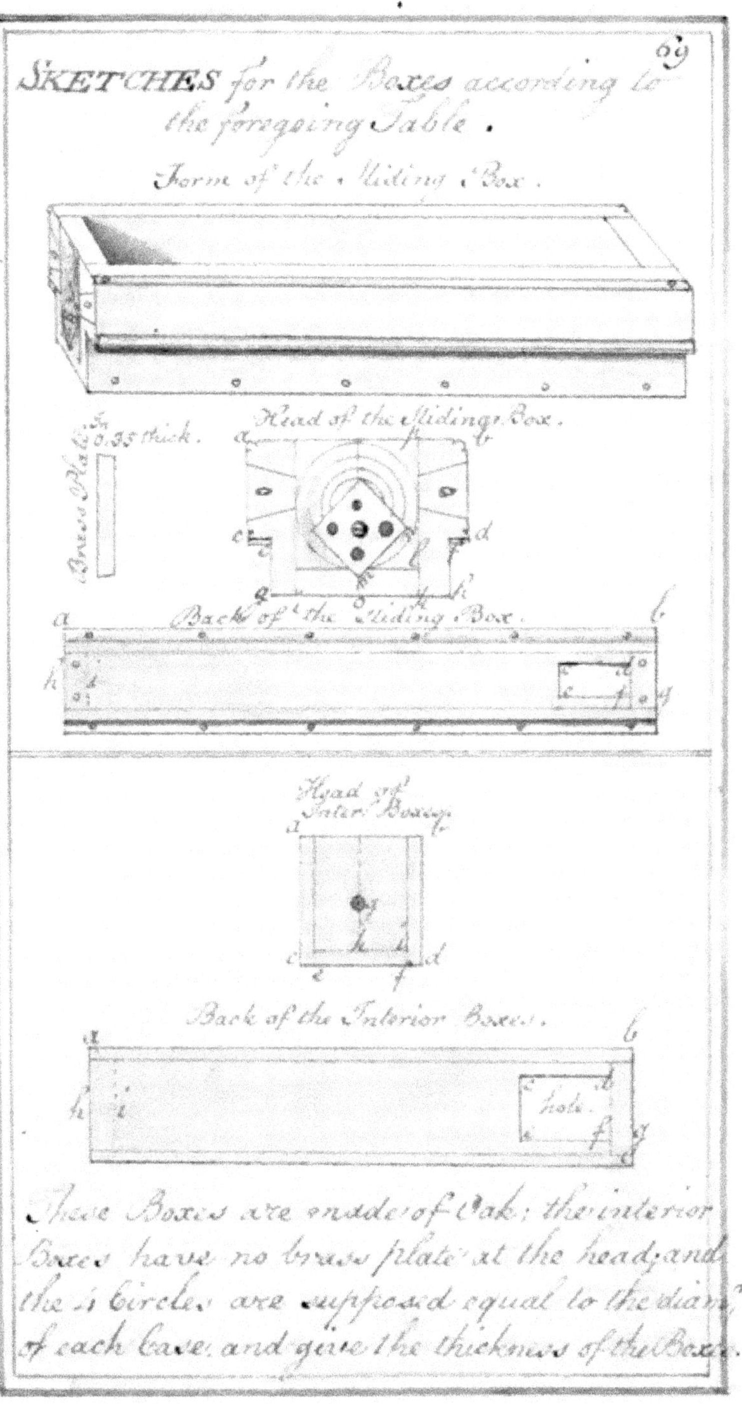
SKETCHES for the Boxes according to the foregoing Table.
Form of the Sliding Box.
Head of the Sliding Box.
Brass Plate In. 0.35 thick.
Back of the Sliding Box.
Head of Inter. Boxes.
Back of the Interior Boxes.
hole.
These Boxes are made of Oak; the interior Boxes have no brass plate at the head, and the 2 Circles are supposed equal to the diam.r of each Case and give the thickness of the Boxes.

7°
To fix the Rockets in the Box for boring there must be a plain loop of strong pack-thread or small line; which being put over the Neck of the Case, the Rocket must be fixt in it's Box close to the head and the other end secured tight with wedges.

Particular Care to be taken to see that the Bitt runs steady and exact to the hole in the brass plate; which should be first tried to see that all is right.

The Holes in the brass plate being adapted to receive it's proper Bitt, the plate must be unscrewed and the corresponding hole turned upwards, according to the Nature of Rockets to be Bored.

In the next place the exact thickness of the head of the Box or Boxes must be measured, and from thence to the mark at 3½ on the Case, this whole length must be sett off very exactly on the Bitt measuring from the tip of the nose and marking at the length with Chalk,

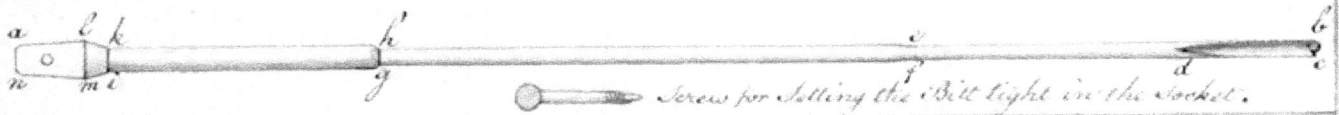

a l k h o b
n m i g f d c

Screw for setting the Bitt tight in the Socket.

TABLE of the Dimensions of Bitts for Boreing of Rockets in the Lathe.

	Lengths.						Diameters.					
	Total Length a b.	a l.	l k.	k h.	h e.	Belly. d c.	a n.	l m.	k i.	h g.	e f.	Vise b c.
	Ft. In. 10	In. 10	In. 10	In. 10	In. 10	In. 10	In. 10	In. 10	In. 10	In. 10	In. 10	In. 10
2 Pou.rs	2:0,15	1,05	...	8,48	5,56	2,7	0,36	0,42	0,29	0,25	0,14	0,16
1 / ½ }	1:8,05	0,64	0,6	7,7	4,6	2,15	0,36	0,42	0,35	0,26	0,12	0,13
¼	1:7,86	0,65	0,29	5,79	3,3	1,65	0,36	0,42	0,32	0,25	0,9	1,65

N. B. The difference between the 1 Pd. and ½ Pd. Bitt is so small, that the 1 Pd. Bitt may very well serve for both, only observing not to Bore the Half Pounder Rockets home by 4/10.

Chalk.

Then the man that turns the Wheel must do it moderately, not too slow nor too swift; the person who attends the Box keeps it pressing forward on the Bitt with the left hand while one can moderately count six, then pushing the Box back clear of the Bitt, he strikes gently ~~on the~~ on the end of the Bitt, with a piece of small round Cane, to clear out the Composition which falls into a box beneath; the pressing the Box forward and clearing the Bitt at each Interval to be repeated till the head of the box is nearly home to the chalk mark on the Bitt; the wedges then to be taken out, and the Rocket pulled out of the box by the loop; emptying the loose composition out of the Rocket into the receiving box, placing the bored Rocket in a basket or box; the Method is exactly the same for Boring each Rocket.

14: 20 and 50 Pound Rockets were

drove

drove on an iron Spindle, it's length equal to half the length of the Bore of the Rocket and hollow drifts to that height; this method of driving especially in large Cases is dangerous, except to those skilled in the Method; so that these Rockets were not Bored, but only Reamed up to the 3½ diameters after driving.

Boreing of 2 P.r Signal Rockets.

After they have been first Bored to the 3½ diameters, the measurement must be taken from the open end to the top of the Composition just thro' the Clay,

a b 3½

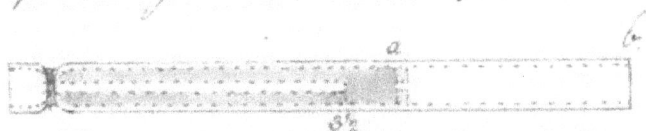

Now according to this Sketch, supposing the Rocket to be first bored to 3½ diameters; then the measurement from the top of the Composition at a to the end of the Case at b must be taken allowing about ½ a tenth of an inch more, to this must be added the thickness of the head of the Boxes and the whole length marked on the Bitt with Chalk as before; then the method of Boreing is 'tis the same, only here the open end of the Rocket at b must be put next to the head of the Box; the whole intention here is only to bore just thro the Clay to touch the Composition that there may be a Communication to the corn powder which forms the Report.

All bounced Sky Rockets to be orderd in the same manner.

N. B. without Clay the Report would be but weak.

To Bounce 2 Pou.^d Sky Rockets for Signals: Corn Powder to be put in sufficient to fill the Case within an inch and half of the top, then the inward folds of paper to be turned down all round on the powder with a flat pointed pricker, about half the thickness of paper may be turned down, then the Case taken to the Choking Engine and choked quite close at top; this being done, ease off the Choking line, and secure the Choke as quick as possible with good pack-thread straining it tight with an old wood Cutter giving six or seven good hitches

one

one after another then cut of the ends almost close.

Then with a sharp knife pare all round the paper at top in form of a button, not taking off too much, and moistning the end a little with the mouth, with a small Mallet beat it down close and handsome all round; each Rocket to be ordered in the same manner.

The Rocket Bounced and Choked.

The Rocket Compleated with it's Button.

It is hoped these Sketches will fully explain the foregoing Method.

Each Rocket must then be furnished with a small paper Cone, equal in diameter at base to the diameter of a Case, and one diameter in length; these are set on by pasting the notched edges of the tube paper of the Cone and then placing them as perpendicular on the head of the Rockets as the eye can judge; a narrow slip of pasted blue paper to be put round, both to strengthen and

and to cover the setting on of the Cone.

When dry, they may be laid up in Store in a dry place; and when any Number is wanted, all that is required is only to Ream them up and tie them upon the Sticks and then they may be packed in boxes.

One Point should be observed for all Rockets, which is, that a circle of tube paper should be pasted on the mouth of each Rocket, before they are put in Store, both to keep out the Air and as a preventive against outward accidents.

As the Method of Making the paper Cones for heading of Rockets will be fully explained further on, these will be inserted with them.

Method of Ordering the Cases for heading and Making Cylinders and Cones.

First the Rockets are to be cut off at the top of the Clay, and this should be done as even as possible; for which purpose it is necessary to have a Cylinder of wood turned to fit exactly on a Case; the Cylinder being set exactly to the Mark, and the knife held.

held steady at the end of the Cylinder all round will cut off the Case even.

Form of the Wood Cylinder for Cutting off the Cases even.

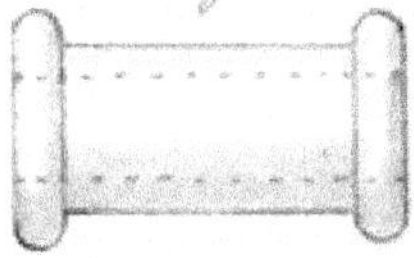

The Case & Cutter of Wood fixt to its Mark.

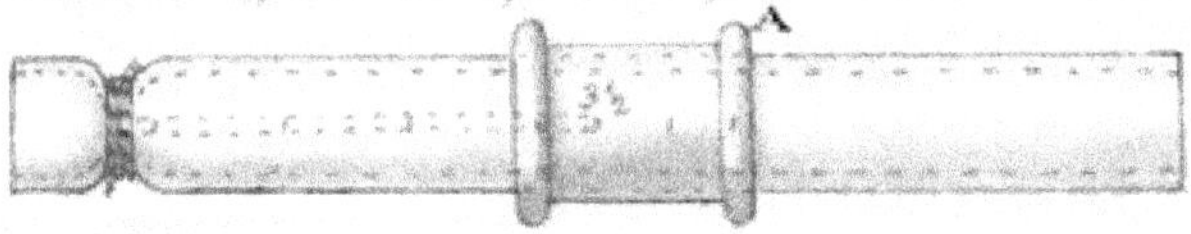

A

$3\frac{1}{2}$

According to the above Sketch, it is only to place the knife at a, and pressing on the knife, let the Case and Cutter turn round under the left hand, setting the knife fresh on again at each extent.

After the Cases are cut off, a small hand Bitt may be used to Bore just through the Clay to the composition at top.

As some Cases will be a small matter less than others, and consequently the Cutter will not sit tight on them, to remedy this, let a slip of paper or small wedge of wood be set in to keep it steady.

The following Table gives proportions for the Cylinders and Cones for Heading.

TABLE of the Proportion of Cylinders and Cones for Heading of Sky Rockets.

Nature of Rockets.	Wooden Rings.			Cylinder	Cone.
	Diam.r Exterior	Thickness	Inter.r Diam.r	Height 2 Diam.rs	Height 2 Diam.rs
	AB	EF	CD	GH	GH
Pounders	In.s 10,ths	In.s 10,ths	In.s 10,ths	In.s 10,ths	In.s 10,ths
50 ...	8,31	1,24	6,00	12,46	12,46
20 ...	6,12	0,90	4,30	.9,18	.9,18
14 ...	5,43	0,81	3,80	.8,14	.8,14
.6 ..	4,09	0,61	2,80	.6,14	.6,14
.4 ...	3,57	0,53	2,48	.5,36	.5,36
.2 ...	2,84	0,42	2,00	.4,26	.4,26
.1 ..	2,25	0,34	1,50	.3,38	.3,38
.½ ...	1,79	0,26	1,187	.2,68	.2,68

N.B. The Diameter of the Cylinders will be as the exterior of the Wood Rings, and the Bases of the Cones the Same.

The Wood Rings are turned out of Fir.

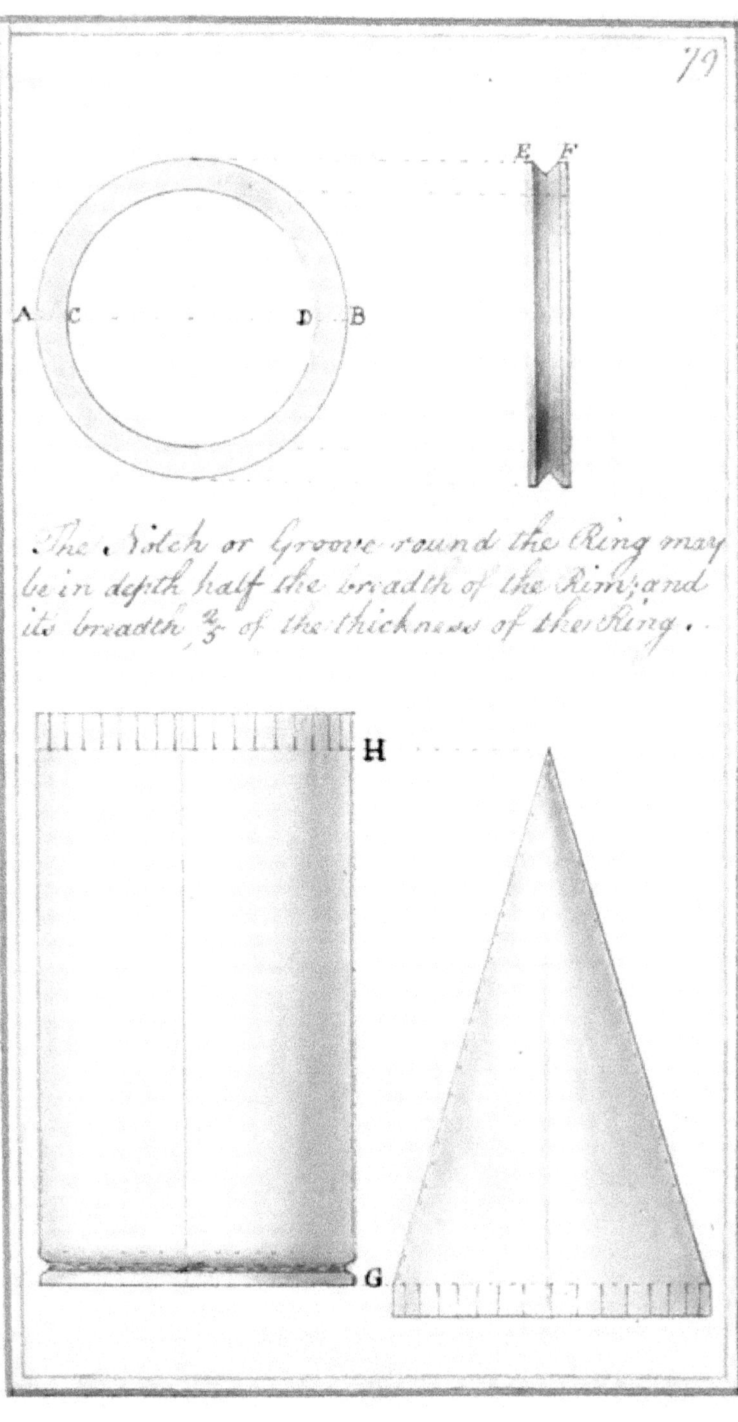

79
E
F
A
C
D
B
The Notch or Groove round the Ring may be in depth half the breadth of the Rim; and its breadth 2/5 of the thickness of the Ring.
H
G

Method of Making the Cylinders.

First it will be necessary to calculate the circumference by the diameter of the Ring, which may be easily done by the common proportions of 7 to 22 or 113 to 355, which will give the length of paper, to which must be added ½ an inch more for lapping over; there were Patterns for each Nature formerly.

Again for the Breadth of the paper, the length or height of Cylinder including the Ring is two exterior diameters of the Rocket, but the paper must be cut half an inch wider to allow for choking it into the groove of the Ring.

We shall only consider the 1 Pounders and half Pounders in this view.

Form of the Pattern of Cartridge Paper.

Form of the Pattern of Tube or Indent paper.

Cylinder Former. Cone Former.

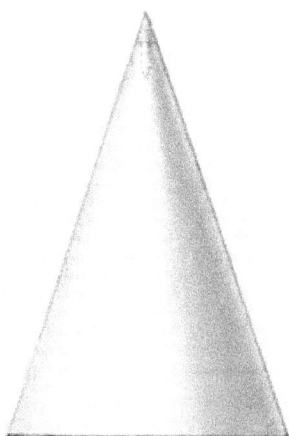

These are usually turned out of well seasoned Beech or Ash wood.

The Apex or point of the Cone Former should be of Brass or Copper set in.

From the foregoing Explanations it will be easy to proportion the Formers, Cylinders and Cones to any Stature of Rockets required.

To Make or Form the Cylinders.

The Patterns of Cartridge and tube paper being Cut out (a sufficient number) place a Ring on the end of the Former and roll up one of the patterns of Cartridge paper on the Cylinder Former, then pasting the inside of the part that laps over, set it close down by pressing it nile with the fingers, then with the small brush paste all over the Cartridge paper and roll the tube paper on it letting the notched part be above the end of the Cartridge paper, and as before lay down the overlap with a little paste, and having a length of fine packthread fastned to a staple drove in a convenient place, at the other end of the packthread an old cutting stick) with this the paper must be choked close into the groove of the Ring all round and immediately tied down with two turns of fine twine.

This is the general Method of making the

the Cylinders, only observing that,

In choking, to hold the paper tight to the Former, that the paper may not vary at the upper end but only at the Ring end; what paper remains above the Ring must be cut close all round with a pair of scissors.

The Rings should be turned a twelvemonth before they are used, on account of shrinking; when they are new they are apt to shrink from the paper tho' ever so well choked, by which means some Rockets set fire to their Heading before they have got up half their height.

The Cylinders as compleated, to be set on tables to dry; there should be a number of each Nature always ready in Store.

For Cones.

The Pattern of paper is formed by the Sector of a Circle, equal to the Base and altitude of the Cone, allowing half an inch or more in proportion for the lap.

The Method of making the Cones is

the

the same as for Cylinders, Viz.t a pattern of Cartridge paper and a pattern of tube paper to each; taking particular care to close the apex or point at top.

The tube paper of the Cylinders and Cones may be laid on whole, then trimmed and notched after they are dry.

Pattern of Cartridge paper for Cones.

a .... b

Pattern of tube Paper.

		In.s 10ths
For 1 Pounders	Length of perpendicular	3, 4.
	Diameter a b	6, 0.
For 1/2 Pounders	Length of perpendicular	2, 7.
	Diameter a b	4, 9.

The indent or tube Patterns are cut a little larger, about 6/10 of an inch for the notched part; Indent paper is preferable to tube paper.

Having a number of Cylinders and Cones in readiness; the Rockets must be made to receive the Cylinders as follows,

Take a Rocket bored and cut to it's proper length, and placing the wood Cylinder exactly

at

at the lower mark for the thickness of the Clay, score lightly all round the Case at the end of the Cylinder with a knife, let the Cylinder be taken off, and with the knife continue to cut all round exactly by the same mark to take off the outward fold of paper; then try a Cylinder to see if the Ring will go on; if not, take off a little more paper equally all round till the Ring of the Cylinder fits on tight, leaving the Cylinder on when fitted; Each Rocket to have a Cylinder fitted on it in the same manner.

The wood Cylinder is used to score true round the Case, that the paper Cylinder may sit on even.

Each Rocket being fitted with a Cylinder it will be necessary to have a pot of hot glue with a small stick flat at one end in it, then take a Rocket and pull off the Cylinder, next with the stick glue round the cut neck of the Rocket, immediately fixing on the Cylinder with a quick turn; Each Rocket to have it's Cylinder glued on in the same manner.

Care

Care to be taken in running the glue round the neck, not to let any run over the Clay into the hole at top, for that would stop the Communication.

When the Rockets have stood 2 hours for the glue to dry, they will be fit for Heading.

Method of Heading Sky Rockets.

Take the Ladle for driving the Rockets with, and put a ladlefull of mealed powder into each Cylinder, preparing a dozen or two, then the Stars or Rains to be put in so as just to fill each Cylinder to the top.

There are various kinds of Stars for Heading of Rockets; As, Rolled Stars; Mould Stars; Blind Stars; Gold Rain, with many more; the Method of Making and ordering them will be inserted further on.

To proceed with Heading, after the Cylinders are filled with Stars or Rains there must be a circle of Cartridge paper

put

put on the top of each, then the inside of the notched paper at top of the Cylinder to be pasted with the fingers all round and laid down upon the circle of Cartridge paper to secure the Heading, then set to dry for half a day.

The Circles of Cartridge paper are equal in diameter to the Cylinder Former, and stampt out with proper steel punches.

Sketch of the Method for pasting down the notched paper on the Circle of cartridge paper to secure the Heading.

When dry the Cones are to be placed on by pasting the inside of the notched paper at the base of the Cone all round; particular care to be taken to set on the Cone as perpendicular as possible the eye can judge then set to dry; and when dry a slip of pasted blue paper to be put on all round

round to hide the setting on of the Cones.

When dry the Rockets may be Reamed carefully to the full Bore.

The next Article consists in tying them on the Sticks, which is very easy only observing to pull the packthread tight at the upper part next the Cylinder where the Composition is solid, but in bringing it down round the Choke care must be taken not to pull too tight, which might break away the Composition round the neck and spoil the Rocket.

In general, three turns of packthread round the top and three turns round the Choke are sufficient for tying on Quarter Pound and Half Pound Rockets and four turns for One Pounders.

They may then be packt in proper Boxes.

From many Experiments made on 20 lb Rockets, the following Proportions are the best.

	Callibers
Length of Composition drove	4,425
Length Bored	3,700
Dead Head	0,725
Height of Clay	0,200
Elm Tampion fixt with glue	0,375

N.B. One of these Rockets fired at Woolwich in November 1752 was a very fine one; the Height taken by two Quadrants appeared to be 1265 Yards.

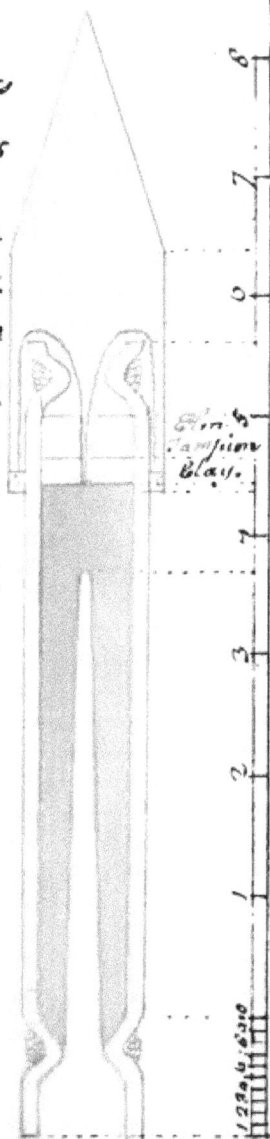

Elm Tampion
Clay.

Scale of Callibers for this 20 Pdr. Each Calliber being 4,39 Inches.

96

This is the true Proportion from a Half to a Six Pounder, and the whole Length of the Rocket headed with it's Cylinder and Cone is exactly 9 Callibers and $\frac{1}{3}$ of a Calliber; the Choke is $\frac{2}{3}$ of a Calliber and the thickness of Paper set off from the upper turn of Packthread to Measure from ~

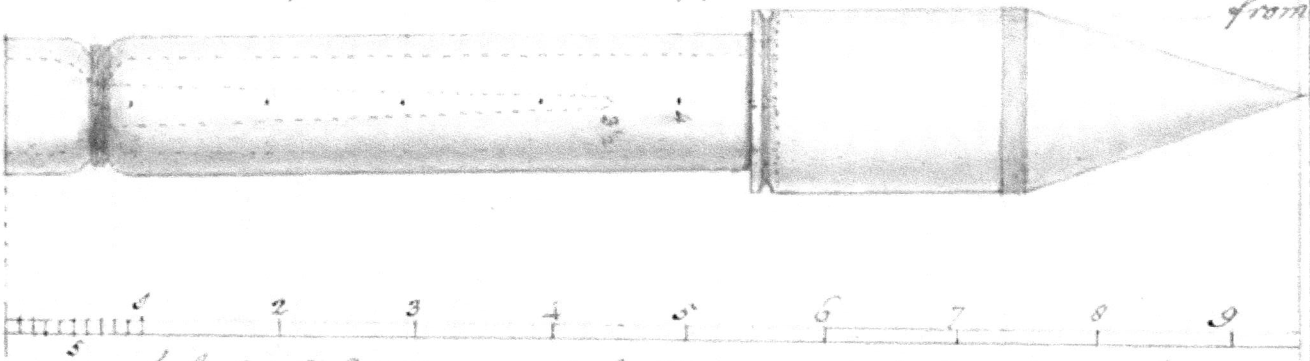

4

3½

1 2 3 4 5 6 7 8 9

5

A Scale of Callibers, each Calliber equal the Diam^r. of the Rocket.

Quarter Pound Sky Rockets are only used in Flights of two or four dozen each; formerly they were Bounced exactly in the same manner as the two Pounder Signal Rockets; but make a better appearance when headed with Stars according to these Sketches.

Pattern of whitey brown Paper

5½ In.

10½ In.

for making the Cap

4

3½

3

¼ Pound Rocket ready for Capping.

3½

3

¼ Pound Rocket compleatly Capped & headed with Stars; total length from end to end 13 Inches.

To make the Caps on Quarter-pound Rockets, is only to paste about an inch of each paper along the bottom and at one end, pasting a dozen or two in the same manner.

Then a Rocket being held in the left hand, place the pasted edge of a paper to the mark at 3 on the Rocket and having made a little more than one turn round the Case, turn the Case round with the left hand and holding the end of the paper with the right hand till it is all rolled up; then let the edge be secured with a little more paste if necessary.

As the Rockets are capped let them be set in a tray or box to dry for a day or two.

When dry, two or three dozen may be set upright in a box, and then a two ounce ladlefull of dry mealed powder put into each Case.

Then

Then 16 middle sized mould Stars to be put into each Cap, but the Stars should be all of one Mould, or else the Caps will not be equally filled.

Next the Caps are to be drawn close or choked just above the Stars with a small line having one end fastned to a staple and at the other end a short stick of round wood to pull by the chokes to be tied down with three or four turns of coarse twine in the usual manner, then the top of the paper above the Choke to be moderately pared away and gently beat down in form of a Button, which compleats them for tying on the Sticks.

There are two forms of Fixing these Rockets for Flights, Viz.^t Rocket Chests and Fan Chests; In the Chests the Rockets ascend perpendicular; but in the Fan Chests they rise in all directions because the bottom of these Chests is much narrower than the top. The

The following Sketches of the Rocket and Fan Chests are according to the Laboratory Method.

Rocket Chest.

Fan Chest.

Front.

In.
21,8

Side.

Thickness of Back and Front ½ an inch; thickness of Side 5/8.

Explanation for the Rocket & Fun Chests.

The Rocket Chests contain 49 Rockets each; the upper Board must be laid with Quickmatch all along each Row of holes and all round the outside square the Quickmatch to be secured with small tacks; to place the Rockets in the Chests there must be two men, one to put the Rockets in at top and the other to guide the ends of the Sticks through their proper hole in the lower Board, for this purpose it is handiest to lean the Chest back upon a tressel. the Rockets being all in, the lid or top must be shut and secured with four or five turns of good packthread round two nails, one drove in the lid and the other near the top of the front for that purpose.

When these Chests are placed where they are to stand for Firing, the strings must be cut to set the lids at liberty, and just before they are to be fired

fired, the Lids must be flung open with the end of a stick by men stationed for that purpose, when a Portfire stuck over the top will instantly discharge them.

For the Fan Chests, the Board must be laid with Quickmatch so along each Row of holes and all round the square secured with small tacks; in the front is a hole even with the top of the Board; a short varnished leader about 3 inches long must be prepared with double Quickmatch as in this Sketch

the short quickmatched end must be capped with a slip of varnished tube paper; the other end of the leader must be introduced so far through the hole that it's quickmatch may lay upon the quickmatch on the Board; then the end of the Leader to be gently bent down in front and secured with a tack drove through the leader at about half

half an inch from the hole, then all round the hole about an inch, and over the leader a little beyond the head of the tack must be secured with pasted double tube paper, laid on one after the other for two or three thicknesses, and when dry to be varnished.

Then the Rockets may be put in, and tops cut out of cartoon paper exactly to fit the top of the Chests, these tops are to be secured with slips of pasted double tube paper about two inches broad, laying one half of the breadth upon the wood, and bringing the other over the edge of the cartoon all round, pressing it close down every where with the fingers, and when dry they must be varnished.

The Rockets ought to be primed in the following manner with short pieces of waste quickmatch and mealed powder mixed up with stiff gum water.

A small bit of the Composition to be taken up with the end of the finger and pressed upon the Quickmatch.

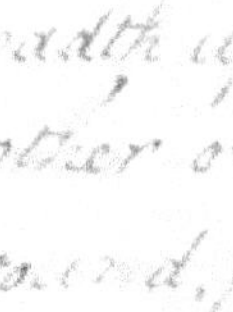

The

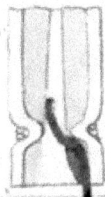

The back of the Fan Chest is furnished with two iron straps which go over upon a cross piece of Fir fixed to an upright

Back of the Chest.

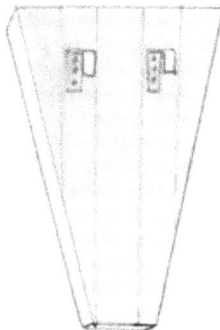

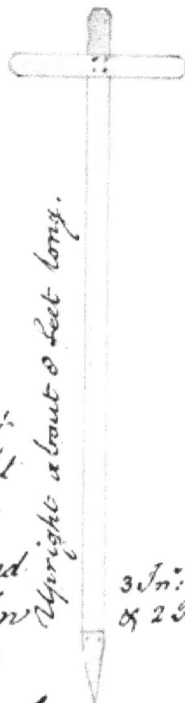

Upright about 8 feet long.

3 In: broad & 2 In: thick

When the Ground will not permit to drive the upright a hole must be dug about a foot or 18 Inches deep and the earth rammed in again all round to keep the Post steady and as perpendicular as possible; the Chests are then to be hitched on the cross piece by means of the iron straps which should go on a little tight.

When they are to be fired, the Cap must be pulled off the end of the Leader.

a b

DIMENSIONS of Reamers for Rockets.

Nature of Rockets.	Diam.r of Reamer at the Choke b.	Diam.r of Reamer at taper end a.	Length of Reamer from a to b.
	In.s 10;ths	In.s 10;ths	Ft. In.s 10;ths
50 Pound.s	1,865	0,5595	1:9,8005
20	1,3737	0,4122	1:4,0605
14	1,2175	0,3050	1:2,2405
6	0,9187	0,2757	0:10,7405
4	0,8025	0,24675	0:9,3800
2	0,6370	0,1920	0:7,4505
1	0,5057	0,15153	0:5,9105
½	0,4000	0,1200	0:4,6900
¼	0,3170	0,0960	0:3,7100

It must be Observed, that the Length of the Reamer from a to b here given, is only 3½ diameters, viz.t from the mark at 3½ to the lowest Mark or setting off above the Choke, to this must be added the length from the lower mark to the immediate [illegible] the Choke; which can best be taken from a well made Case.

Case.

To Use the Reamer: take a Rocket that is bored and measure from the point of the Reamer the whole length from 3½ diameters to the bottom of the Rocket; there making a mark on the Reamer with Chalk.

Hold the Rocket in the left hand point upwards, and the Reamer in the right hand, enter the point carefully, and turn the Reamer steadily and gently round, pressing but little against the Reamer, sometimes taking out the Reamer and emptying the loose composition from the Rocket and Reamer into a Leather bottom or sheet of brown paper; so continuing to Ream out an inch or two at a time, till the chalk mark on the Reamer is exactly even with the bottom of the Case.

At

At every Rocket, the Reamer must be measured, to see if the chalk mark answers exactly to [illegible]; if not, the mark must be altered accordingly; or if rubbed out, marked afresh.

The reason of measuring the Reamer to each Rocket, is on account of being sure, and likewise because a small difference may happen to be in the length of the Chokes of some Rockets.

All the Reamings to be saved, as it must be used to drive the [illegible] for heading of Rockets.

Reaming is both expeditious and easy with proper care, and should be done after the Cylinders are glued on and dry: for if done after the Rockets are compleated it is apt to disturb the Heading.

TABLE of the Length and Proportion for Rocket Sticks.

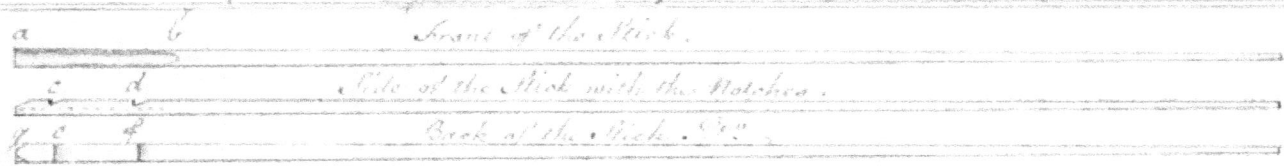

a b Front of the Stick.

c d Side of the Stick with the Notches.

f e d Back of the Stick. &c.

Pounders.	Total Length.	Breadth at Top.	Thickness at Top.	Square at Bottom.	Size at
	Feet : Ins.	Ins. 10ths	Ins. 10ths	Ins. 10ths	Diameter.
6	14 „ 11	1 . 85	1 , 5	0 , 75	1½
4	13 „ 0	1 , 40	1 , 25	0 , 625	1½
2	10 „ 4	1 , 00	1 , 125	0 , 515	1½
1	8 „ 2	0 , 80	0 , 725	0 , 375	1½
½	6 „ 6	0 , 70	0 , 5	0 , 35	1½
¼	5 „ 2	0 , 55	0 . 3753	0 , 25	1½

Remarks on the foregoing Table.

The Length of the Hollow a b, for the Rocket to lay in, 7 diameters.

The Depth of the Hollow; divide the thickness (not the breadth) of the Stick at top into 3½ parts; the depth to be one part.

Depth of the notches c & d, equal to the depth of the Hollow.

From g the top of the Stick, to e the first Notch, half a diameter.

From e to f, (the distance between the two Notches,) 4 diameters and ½ of a diameter.

By the Poize is to be understood, that a diameter and a half being marked off (from the extremity of the mouth of the Rocket) upon the Stick, and there placed on the back of a knife or the finger, the Rocket end and taper end should be in Equilibrio, after the Rocket is tied on; however

however it is proper that the taper end of the Stick stand rather inclining, as the Rockets will thereby ascend more steadier even in a calm night: but if there happens any wind and the Sticks light, the wind will take hold of the taper ends of the Sticks, and thereby force the Rockets far out of a perpendicular.

When Rocket Sticks are prepared for Store, a Year or two beforehand they must not be finished, but only made plain taper Sticks a little larger every way than the true dimensions, on account of drying and shrinking; if, when required to be finished they should prove too heavy, a little planing will reduce them to the proper standard.

Rocket Sticks are generally made out of clean yellow fir.

Account of Fir plank, clean yellow Deal, proper for Rocket Sticks.

Rockets	Length of Plank	Breadth of Plank	Thickness of Plank	Price per foot	No. of Sticks cut out of each Plank	No. of Sticks made by 1 Man in one day
Pounders	Ft. In.	Inc.	Inc.	S. D.	No.	No.
6 } double	16:0	9	....	0:8	8	
4 } Deal	14:0	8	....	0:6	9	
2 } whole	12:0	8	....	0:4	10	
1 } Deals	10:0	7	....	0:3	10	
1/2 } 1 Inc. Deal	14:0	7	1	0:2½	30	
1/4 } slit Deal	12:0	7	½	0:2	32	

Estimate of the Value of Compleating Sky Rockets of each Pixture with Sticks Mens Labour exempted.

	Pou.rs	S.d
Sky Rockets Compleated with Sticks.	6 headed with Stars &c.	5:6
	4 Ditto	4:4
	2 Ditto with Stars or Rains	2:3
	2 Bounced	1:6
	1 headed with Stars	1:6
	1 Do. with Rains	1:8
	1 Bounced	1:3
	1/2 headed with Stars	0:9
	1/2 Do. with Rains	0:10
	1/2 Bounced	0:6
	1/4 Capped with Stars	0:6
	1/4 Bounced	0:4

Estimate of the Expence of Men's Labour for a Sky Rocket of each Nature at 1/6 ℔ diem.

Pou.ᵈˢ	d
6	8.
4	6.
2.	5½.
2	5.
1	4.
1	4.
1	3½.
½	2½.
½	2½
½	2.
¼	1½.
¼	1.

These Calculations are as near as possible when Powder and Petre were not so high; but as the Price of those Articles is increased, a further Allowance must be made in proportion.

The Method of tying the Rockets on to the Sticks is much easier learnt by seeing two or three tied on, than by a description, which would require many Sketches.

Remarks on tying; at the upper notch, the packthread may be pulled pretty tight, but at the lower notch or Choke gently tight for fear of breaking away the Composition at the Neck.

Two Pounder Rockets must have five turns of packthread both at the upper and lower notch; One Pounder Rockets, four turns; Half and Quarter Pound Rockets, three turns.

There are three sorts of packthread viz. fine; Middling and coarse; the fine is used for tying on Quarter and half Pounders; the Middling for One and Two Pounders; and the Coarse or small Line for Four and Six Pounders.

Stars for Sky Rockets.

First to begin with the Laboratory Composition, which makes good Stars.

Rolled Stars.

	lb:oz:dr.
Salt Petre - - - - - - -	4:0:0.
Sulphur - - - - - - -	2:0:0.
Antimony - - - - - -	2:0:0.
Singlass dissolved - -	0:1:12.
Spirits of wine - - -	qts. - 2.
Vinegar - - - - - - -	qts. - 2.

To Mix the Composition; Dissolve a Pound of Singlass, in two Quarts of water by Boiling: the Petre, Sulphur and Antimony to be sifted four times altogether through a hair Sieve to mix it; then put it into a glazed earthen pane; put the above weight of the Singlass jelly into a small pot or pan and pour vinegar over it, stirring them well till the Singlass is dissolved, put this to the dry Composition and stir it well together with

a

a wooden spatula, adding spirits of wine and vinegar a little at a time, till the Composition is brought by working to a stiff paste; then put some of the Composition upon a flat board and cut it into small pieces of different sizes these are to be Rolled into round Balls between the Palms of the hands, then rolled all over in dry mealed powder, and next laid in wooden trays, like butchers' trays, to dry for a fortnight or three weeks, and when dry to be packed up in Barrels with Covers for Store.

These are to be made some of the size of small marbles, some larger, and some as large as a middling Walnut.

It is proper to Make a large quantity of these for Store, as five or six Barrels full.

The smallest Stars are used for small Rockets, &c; but in general they may be used promiscuously.

These are only used for Rockets & Pots de Brins

Laboratory Drove Stars.

	lb:oz.
Salt Petre	[illegible]
Sulphur	2:0
Mealed Powder	1:8.
Antimony	0:4.

To be Sifted altogether four times through a hair Sieve: and to be drove in Portfire cases exactly as for Portfires; then to be cut into lengths of 1 1/2 or 2 inches, and primed at each end with mealed powder mixt with spirits of wine.

Used sometimes for Sky Rockets and Air-Balloons.

This and the foregoing are white.

Gold Rain.

	lb:oz.
Mealed Powder	2:8.
Salt Petre	3:0.
Sulphur	1:8.
Antimony	2:0.
Sea coal dust	1:0.

To be Sifted altogether four times thro' a hair Sieve: then to be mixt up to a

stiff

stiff paste with gum arabic water, and to be Rolled into small Stars about the size of a hazel nut; then rolled in dry mealed powder and put in trays to dry for a fortnight or three weeks.

Effect: Sky Rockets headed with these Stars, shew nothing till some time after the Rocket is expended, when these Stars discover themselves, at about 100 yards from the ground in a fine shower of a gold colour which occupies a large space and descends gently to the ground.
— Curious but not used in common.

Blind Stars.

These are drove in small or large Portfire Cases cut to a proper length;

The Compositions for driving them with, are, the common Fuze Composition, and the Blind Fuze Composition, drove as Fuzes.

The following are the Proportions for them

them.

No. 1.

Fuze.	Blind.	Fuze

No. 2.

Fuze.	Blind.	Fuze.

No. 3.

Fuze.	Blind	Fuze.	Blind.	Fuze.

No. 1 and 2 are intended to light only at one end, the other end must have a Bottom turned in close as for Portfire Cases.

No. 3. is to light at both ends; the ends of each which are to take fire, must be primed with mealed powder mixt up with spirits of wine.

These Stars are proper for loading one Pound Rockets with; after the first shew of Stars, they disappear while the Blind fuze Composition lasts, and then strike out again into Stars, which has a good Effect.

Not used in Common.

Mould

Mould Stars.

These require a long description on Account of the Moulds, and there-fore last in Order.

The Moulds consist of beech handles with a moveable brass ferule to each; their construction is very simple.

Brass Ferule.

Beech Handle.

According to this Sketch; the beech handle has a short nipple with a brass pricker at one end, on this end the brass Ferule is put to form the Stars in; the other end of the handle is a little longer than the brass ferule, and it's use is to push the Star (out of the ferule or Mould,) after it is formed.

There are four sizes of these Stars Viz.t the smallest are ½ of an inch in diameter

diameter and ¼ of an inch high or deep, in these the Gold Rain may be formed.

The 2.^d Size, 4/10 in diameter and 3/10 deep.

The 3.^d Size, 5/10 in diameter and 4/10 deep.

The 4.th Size, 6/10 of an inch in diameter and ½ an inch deep.

It is evident from these dimensions that the length of the brass Ferule and short nipple must be so adapted, as to leave a proper vacancy in the ferule, according to the depth and diameter of each Size.

Composition for Mould Stars.

	lb : oz
Salt Petre	8 : 0.
Sulphur	2 : 0.
Mealed Powder	0 : 8.
Antimony	2 : 0.

To be Sifted altogether four times through a hair Sieve.

To Mix the Composition for making into Stars: previous, it will be necessary to have four or five Gallons of Gum water ready

ready dissolved in a large earthen pan allowing 2 lb of Gum Arabic for each gallon of water.

Then put about ¾ of the sifted Composition into a glazed earthen pan large enough to contain twice the quantity of Composition; about half a pint of the gum water to be put to the Composition in the pan, and then well stirred and worked together with a wood spatula, adding more of the dry Composition, and a little more of the gum water occasionally, working them well together, till the whole is reduced to a stiff paste, stiffer than dough.

Put some of the paste upon a flat board 8 or 9 inches square, then take a mould, the brass ferule on the pricker end, and holding it in the right hand dig at the side of the Composition with a drawing stroke, letting the bottom of the

the ferule rub upon the Board at each stroke, the better to compress the Composition into the ferule, which being full, take off the ferule, and with the other end of the handle push out the composition or Star into dry mealed powder, immediately replacing the ferule and continuing to do as before.

Five or six Strokes are sufficient for one filling.

Seven Men are required for this work, Viz.^t four to fill; Two, to roll the Stars in the mealed powder, to take them out and place them in flat wood trays, and when any trays are full, to carry them into a large room for drying; One, to Mix and supply the Fillers with Composition, and to oversee the work.

As the Rockets and Air Balloons consume a great number of these Stars, it requires great Quantities for Store, at least two Barrels full of each Size.

The Effect of these Stars is white.

Rains

Rains for heading of Rockets.

Rockets headed in the Laboratory for Fireworks, are only One Pounders and Half Pounders.

One Pound Rockets are headed with six dram Rains.

Half Pound Rockets are headed with four dram Rains.

These small cases & no Roll[illegible] Moulds proper for them.

Dimensions of Moulds for Rains and Squibs.

	Nature of Cases.	Length of the Body of the Moulds.	Interior Diameter of the Moulds.	Height of the Nipple.
	Oz: Dr	In: 10ths	In: 10ths	In: 10ths
Rains & Squibs	2 : 0	6 , 2	0 , 9	0 , 45
	1 : 0	4 , 9	0 , 7	0 , 35
	0 : 8	3 , 9	0 , 5	0 , 25
Rains only	0 : 6	3 , 5	0 , 35	0 , 225
	0 : 4	2 , 2	0 , 3	0 , 2

The Nipples of these two last are flat.

Dimensions of Cases for Rains and Squibs.

Nature of Cases	Length of Cases	Diam.r of Cases	Diam.r of Bore	Thickness of Paper	Gauge for Choking.
Oz · dr.	In.s 10ths	In.s 10ths	In.s 10ths	In.s 10ths	In.s 10ths
2 : 0	8 , 0	0 , 800	0 , 5	0 , 195	0 , 5
1 : 0	6 , 0	0 , 640	0 , 45	0 , 120	0 , 45
0 : 8	4 , 0	0 , 400	0 , 375	0 , 057	0 , 375
0 : 6	3 , 125	0 , 348	0 , 225	0 , 061	0 , 301
0 : 4	2 , 5	0 , 290	0 , 2	0 , 048	0 , 25

When these Cases are used for heading of Rockets, they must when compleated, be exactly equal to the interior length of a Cylinder for the Rocket.

The Formers for Rolling these Cases are made of iron; the papers are cut out with a proper slope, in the same manner as for Rocket Cases, then Rolled and filled in their Moulds exactly the same.

For Choaking these cases, a small line is made fast at one end to a Staple near the Rolling Table, at the other end of the Line is an old collar of wood to

which

which the Line is fastned through a hole bored in the middle of the Cutter.

The Workman is furnished with a leathern Belt, which buckles round, and has a strong iron ring fixed to it; when required to Choke, the wood Cutter is to be hitched into the iron ring and the line being put round the Case, the line is pulled tight or slacked by means of the Belt round the waist; the method is in Effect the same as for larger Cases in the Choking Engine, only here, so much strength is not required.

The two Ounce, One Ounce, and half Ounce Cases must have a vent exactly equal to ⅓ of their Bore; for which reason, it will be necessary to have Nipples of hard wood, brass or iron to form the Chokes by.

All the chokes of these Cases to be tied down or secured with five or six hitches of coarse twine.

In short, for the 2, 1 and ½ Ounce cases there must be, Gauges of wood, Cutters of wood; Iron, brass or wood Nipples for Choking, and after the Choke is made the Case to be put on its Nipple with the Former and three or four strokes given with the Mallet on the head of the former to set down the Choke, after which the Case is to be cut to its proper length by the Gauge.

The 6 and 2 dram Cases are choked quite close at one end, having no other Vent than their Bore.

2 dram Case.

The 6 dram Cases are made in the same form, and both are to be drove full with Composition, then primed with mealed [illegible] of [illegible] of [illegible]

the [illegible] 4 dram cases are not Bounced.

[illegible] of paper to roll [illegible]

[illegible] the forms of the 2, 1, and half ounce cases.

Form of the case.

The case drove and Bounced Compleat.

The 2 and 1 ounce Cases are usually made of Cartridge Paper; the ½ Ounce, 6 and 4 dram cases may be made of indent, or any waste paper stiff enough.

From the Sketches it may be easily inferred that the Method of Rolling these Cases differs from Rocket Cases only in size and the lengths; and the Method of Bouncing is exactly the same as for those fixed Rockets.

It has been Observed, the [illegible]

and

and Reamings from the Rockets must be saved, and are to be used for driving these Cases, and is [illegible] Rains with.

These small Cases are to be drove with Sky Rocket Composition; and the 2 and 1 Ounce Cases, when used for heading of Rockets, may be drove with the following Composition; Viz!

	lb: oz.
Salt Petre	2 : 0.
Charcole	0 : 12.
Sulphur	0 : 4.
Mealed Powder	0 : 12.

The Petre and Charcole to be well rubbed together between the hands, and then add the rest, sifting all together thro' a hair Sieve four times.

TABLE for driving of Rains, for heading Rockets.

Nature of Rockets	[illegible] of Rains	Nature of Ladle	Nature of Rammers	No. of blows to each ladle full of Composition	Length of Case drove [illegible]	No. of Rains for heading each Rocket	No. of each [illegible]
Pounds	Oz : dr	Ins.	Ins.	Blows.	Ins. 10ths	No.	No.
6	2 : 0	13	8	16	3,5	19	28
4	1 : 0	10	8	12	3,0	19	60
2	0 : 8	8	5½	10	1,75	19	75
1	0 : 6	Cohorn	4⅖	7	full	19	100
½	0 : 4	Hand.	Hand.	5	full	19	150

The capes of all these cases must be primed with mealed powder mixt up with spirits of wine or gum water.

Squibs.

These are only made of two and one Ounce cases, and are drove with corned powder only; the Ladles and Mallets the same as before; only giving 18 strokes to each ladlefull of powder for the 2 Ounce and 14 or 15 strokes for the 1 Ounce; they must be drove hard.

To be drove up to a little more than half the length of the case from the choke, then bore it and prime in the usual manner.

Stands for Rockets.

In the large way, they run 24 feet long, and contain 24 Rockets, Fig! 12 in front, and 12 at the back having one foot interval.

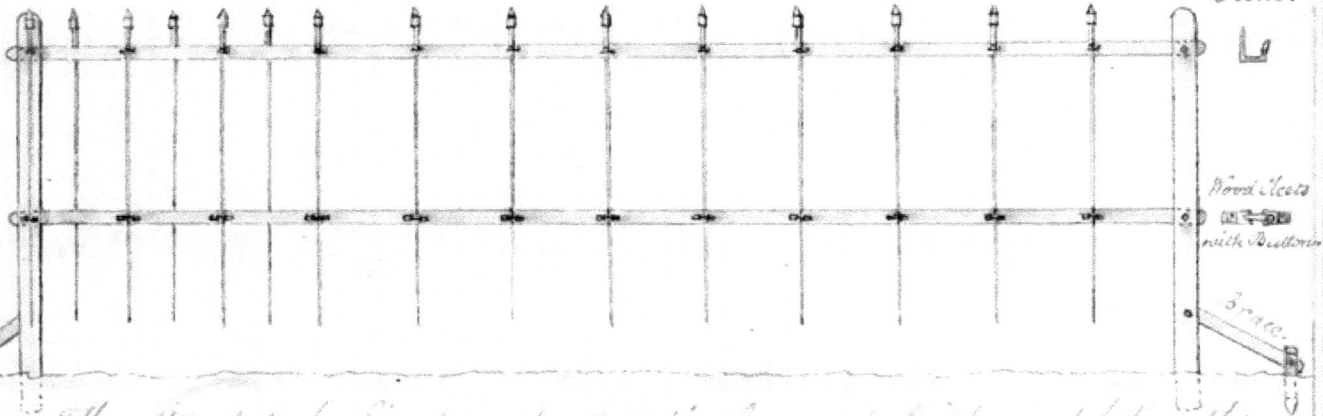

Large Frame or Stand to hang Rockets on, for Firing.

Hook.

Wood Cleets with Buttons

Brace.

The Stand to be fixed as perpendicular as possible; and before the Rockets are hung up, the finger must be forced thro' the Circle of paper at the mouth, to open them for Firing; there are usually three or four Stands at a Firework; Viz^t. Two for half Pound Rockets and Two for One Pound Rockets; there must be Stars and Rains alternately; two Rockets to be fired at a time: one to each Stand.

Stand for a Single Rocket. Stand for 2 Rockets.

Iron Hook.

No 1 No 2

Button, Cleet. Cleet.

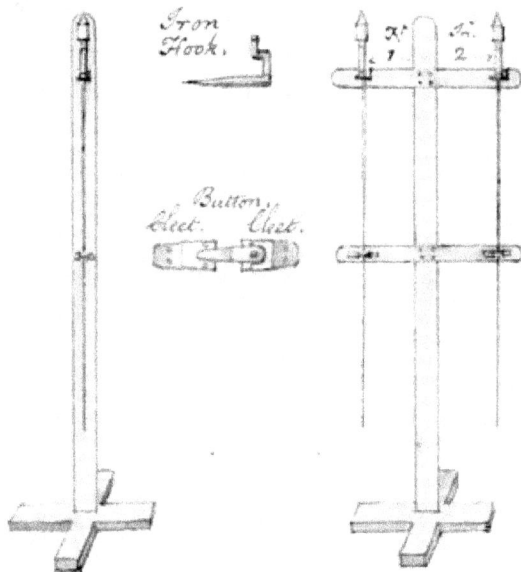

These are only for Experiments; no dimensions are here given, because the Size of the Rockets and Sticks must determine all the rest; great care must be taken, that the hooks are not too narrow any way, but just sufficient for the Rockets to hang freely.

The Cleets; the thickness may be from $\frac{1}{10}$ to $\frac{2}{10}$ more than the thickness of the Stick at that part; and the breadth between the Cleets in proportion, just to allow the Stick free Play, but not too much: for the Rockets will go, as directed by the small end of the Stick.

Extra Heading for Sky Rockets &c.

Girandole Rocket.

Girandole.

Clay. Brilliant. Clay. Brilliant. Clay.

Girandole Rocket.

Suppose the Girandole to be a 2 Ounce Case which is large enough for 1 Pound Rockets. One end must be choked quite close as in the Sketch, then mark off, with the same allowance as for choking at the other end; put the Case into the Mould and drive down One 2 Ounce ladlefull of Clay with 16 strokes of an 8 inch Mallet.

Take the Case out of the Mould, and measure with the drift how far the first ladlefull of Clay fills up from the Choke and mark it on the outside of the Case; set off the same from the allowance for Choke at the other end; then with Compasses or a slip of paper find the Center or middle between the Clay at the ends and mark it; from the middle mark set off ¼ of an inch on each side for the middle Clay; by this mark off the rest of the Cases.

Brilliant

Brilliant for Girandole Cases.

	lb:oz.
Mealed Powder	2:8.
Salt Petre	0:6.
Sulphur	0:2.
Steel or bright iron Filings	0:6

To be sifted altogether 4 times thro' a hair Sieve.

One Ladlefull of Brilliant at a time, and 16 Strokes to each ladlefull with an 8 Inch Mallet; to be Clayed and drove with brilliant at each end, exactly as the foregoing Sketch; then to be choked close at the other end and each end being primed a little, they must be formed into Buttons in the usual manner.

Having completed the number of Cases thus far; Next, with a small Gimblet of $\frac{1}{10}$ of an inch diameter, bore quite thro' the Case, at the Center of the middle Clay; thro' this hole it is to be placed and turn upon its Spindle.

Then at Right angles to the said Center hole and at about $\frac{1}{4}$ of an inch from the Clay at each end, and with a Bit or Gimblet equal to $\frac{1}{3}$ of the diameter of the Bore of the Case; Bore two holes, one at each end, but on opposite sides, Boring only just thro'

thro' the paper to touch the composition.

Girandole Case

Center hole

Back side Vent

Front side Vent

Tube paper double Leader, to communicate from the top of the Rocket, to the Vents of the Case.

The Rocket to be Cut off at the top of the Clay as usual for heading with Stars or Rains. A small hole to be bored thro' the middle of the Clay at top just to touch the Composition.

A slip of tube paper about 2 inches broad and long enough to go 3 times round, to be rolled round the top of the Rocket, so as to form a Cap standing an inch and half above the top of the Rocket, and secured with two or three turns of coarse twine.

A two Ounce ladle full of mealed powder to put into the Cap, and then the double tied end of the leader put in at top of the Clay, and the Cap being gathered close to it all round, tie

tie in the Leader with two or three turns of coarse twine.

Each Rocket to be furnished with a cap, mealed powder at top, and the Leaders tied in, alike; care to be taken to tie the cap tight on at the top of the Rocket, that it may not slip off when tying in the leader.

The Case to be covered all over with single pasted paper, a little below the setting on and a little above the tie on the Leaders.

The Rockets to be tied on the Sticks in the usual manner.

The wire spindles to be fixed firm in the head of the Sticks, about 3 inches above; first put an inch of small leader on the wire, then put on the Girandole Case; and next a waistcoat button Mould convex side down, at a quarter of an inch below the top of the wire, make several tight turns, one over another, to secure the case from working off; produce the ends of the Leader to the respective vents, tying the Leaders to the case as in the Sketch, and finished by pasting over with single paper.

Caduceus Rockets.

These are made of 1 or 2 Pounder Sky Rockets, drove in the usual manner.

The long Sticks are made to 8 square,

1 Pounder — total length of Stick Ft. In. [illegible].0.

Thickness at top ... 0,[illegible].

Length of Cross Stick In. 10,5. Thick In. 0,5,

Breadth D.º In. 0,75.

Rockets distant from Center to Center In. 9,6.

2 Pounder — total length of Stick Ft. In. 12.10.

Thickness at top ... In. 1,0.

Length of Cross Stick In. 12. Thick In. 0,3,

Breadth D.º In. 0,65.

Rockets distant from Center to Center In. 10,5.

N.B. The Cross Stick set through the middle of the long Stick at In. [illegible]0 from the top, then glewed and Nailed.

At the top is a Cap to contain a 1 Ounce Marroon.

At the bottom is a double Leader Quickmatched, communicating to both Rockets.

These and the foregoing are not used in Common.

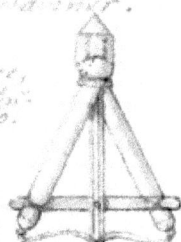

It is hoped this Sketch will be a sufficient Explanation.

N.B. The Leaders in the Sketch are brought down to shew them; but they must be laid along the middle of the Cross Sticks, so as to let the Rockets rise.

LINE ROCKETS.

These may be made of ¼ Pounder; ½ Pounder; 1 Pounder, or 2 Pounder Rockets.

The Cases are made in the usual manner as for Sky Rockets headed with Stars or Rains and of the same length.

The Cases are to be drove with Sky Rocket Composition; only instead of 1/5 of Clay at top, it must be increased to 1/3 of a diameter of Clay.

The Cases to be drove 4½ diameters with Composition; to be Bored and Reamed 3½ diameters and to be cut off at top of the Clay.

This proportion is given where the full extent can be allowed; but where the length of Line must be short, the Rockets must be drove Bored and Reamed in proportion.

For Instance, supposing the extent of a 1 Pounder Rocket to be 300 Yards, and only 200 or 150 Yards can be had, it is evident that the Length of Composition, Boring and Reaming must be in Proportion.

Single

Single and double Line Rockets. we will beg leave to omit the Single; as being the Case.

No. 1. End. a

No. 2. End.

No. 3. End. From the above Sketches it will be easy to manage 4 Cases; a Sketch would be too confused.

No. 1. represents a solid Bracket of Fir, it's length equal to the Rocket, and it's Breadth equal to 2 diameters; the Thickness equal to $\frac{3}{4}$ of the exterior diameter of the Rocket; exactly thro' the middle length must be a hole bored large enough for the Bracket to move freely on the line or Rope it is intended to run on; near the ends are two holes for tying the Rockets firm on with packthread — the Sides must be grooved for the Rockets to lay in.

No. 2. represents a solid Triangular Bracket to contain three Rockets.

No. 3. represents a solid Fir Bracket to contain four Rockets; the Sides for the Rockets must

must be screwed as usual, and the inter-mediate sides hollowed out sufficient to bore the holes for tying on.

The Line may be 32 Pounder used for hoisting Flags &c; either smaller or larger in proportion, so as to bear straining tight; and the Eye should be well greased.

To Fix the Rockets.

The Rockets being drove, Bored, Reamed, and cut off in the usual manner; must be Bored through the middle of the Clay just to touch the Composition; the last Case must not be Bored thro' the Clay.

The Mouths of all the Rockets to be primed with mealed powder mixt up with spirits of wine, and rubbed lightly round the inside of the Cup with the end of the finger.

All the Cases, except the last, must have a Cartouch of tube paper tied on at each end, to receive the leaders which communicate from one Rocket to the other; the last Case to have only one Cartouch at the mouth.

the

The following Sketches it is hoped will make this very plain.

The Rocket Cartouched at both Ends.

The last Rocket or dead Head.

The Cartouches are slips of tube paper about two inches broad, and long enough to go three times round the case; these are to be Rolled on tight at each end, and tied on with coarse twine.

The last Rocket or dead Head, must have the clayed and stopped with double tube paper pasted and a slip put round and pressed close as in the Sketch .... see Frezier.

To Tie on the Rockets.

Place a Rocket in its groove and tie it on with three turns of packthread thro' each hole; observing not to tie it too tight at the Choke of the Rocket the Mouths of the Rockets must be placed contrarywaye or reversed, Viz.t suppose four Rockets, and the mouth of the first placed to the right hand,

then

then the mouth of the second must be [illegible]
to the left hand; the mouth of the third to
the right, and the mouth of the fourth to
the left; so that the two opposite Rockets will
have their mouths stand the same way.

The Rockets being tied on, take slips of
pasted double tube paper about an inch broad
and cover all over the packthread at each
tie, pressing the paper close; then let them
stand to dry for half a day.

In the mean time prepare the leaders
to communicate from one Rocket to the other,
the leaders to be of Cartridge paper and the
Quickmatch that of four threads.

The Leader Quickmatch'd.

A little mealed powder to be put into
the choked end of the first Rocket, then
one end of the leader, gathering the
Cartouch together all round and tie in
the leader; bend the Leader carefully,
and place the other end into the mouth
of the second Rocket, and tie in the

Leader

Leader as before; fixing in all the leaders in the same manner, then paste or cover all the leaders and Cartouches except the first with pasted double tube paper, and set them to dry.

The Line should be well greased and must have a Cushion at each end, as the Rockets strike with great force.

The Effect of these, Running backwards and forwards on the Line, is pretty enough, but never used in the Laboratory, tho' here given.

Several curious Inventions may be formed on this Plan, as, A Mercury with a Stick and lighted Portfire, instead of a Caduceus, flying to give fire to the first piece of Fireworks; A Dragon; A Dove; or any other Device suitable to the Occasion.

To perform these things properly it will be necessary to understand the forming of light Figures, the Method of Fixing and painting Silk in Transparent Colours and

particularly

particularly to adapt the Lights so as not to endanger the figure.

Indeed for Pieces that are only intended to be seen in the day time, external painting and Ornaments are sufficient.

In both Cases, it will be Necessary to adapt the size of the Rockets to that of the Figure and vice versa; when the Figures are heavy, it may be proper to fire two Rockets at a time, or to reinforce the Composition with mealed powder.

It will likewise require weights or pullies, to keep the Figures steady and upright.

Trials ought to be made beforehand, to insure Success.

These Hints it is hoped, are sufficient for an ingenious Person!

Chinese Rockets.

These are 4 Pounder Cases, drove with Chinese Composition, Viz.t

	lb. : oz.
Salt Petre	10 : 0.
Charcole	2 : 0
Sulphur	1 : 4.
Pounded Iron prepared	7 : 4.

The Salt Petre and Charcole to be well rubbed together between the hands; then, the Iron to be spread on a table and a few drops of Spirits of wine added to it, then worked backwards and forwards with a brass Slice till the Iron appears equally damped, then the Sulphur to be added to the Iron and well mixt together with the Slice; the Sulphur and Iron to be added to the Petre and Charcole and the whole well mixt together by rubbing between the hands and working with the Slice.

These Rockets are to be drove on an Iron Spindle and hollow drifts.

The Cases of these Rockets differs from Sky Rockets, in requiring to be something larger; Viz.t supposing the diameter of the

Bore

Bore of the Case to be divided into 6 equal parts; then the Vent at the Choke shall be 3/6 or half the Bore; and the top at 3½ diameters must be 1/6 part, by this the Spindle is to be made.

The length of the Spindle must be exactly equal from the bottom of the Case to the Mark at 3½ diameters.

1/6

3/6

Wood Block with Iron Spindle.

First Case on the Spindle; then put in a ladlefull of Composition as usual, then the long hollow Drift and with a 13 Inch Mallet give 36 smart strokes.

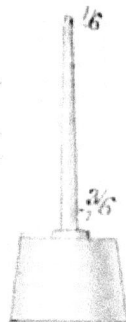

Then the long Drift to be taken out and the hollow end held over the Composition Box, strike on the head of the Drift with the Mallet till the hollow of the Drift is quite clear from Composition; then put in another ladlefull

of

of Composition driving it down; before, take out the long drift and clear it from Composition.

Drive three or four ladlesfull of Compositions with the long drift then take the next long drift for three or four ladlesfull; then use the third hollow drift till the Composition is drove to about a quarter of an inch above the top of the Spindle, which may be known by Measuring.

This last Caution must be particularly attended to; for as the fourth drift is short and solid, was the top of the Spindle to be uncovered, there would be danger either of Splitting the drift, or setting the Case on fire.

These Cautions must be observed for all Rockets drove on Spindles.

These Rockets must be drove on

a

a spindle, as they cannot be bored, when drove, on account of the pounded Iron.

There must be ⅓ of a Callibre of Clay drove at top; then cut off at top of the Clay; bored through the Clay; and headed with Stars or Rains in the same manner as other Sky Rockets.

These Rockets being heavier on account of the Iron, require a larger bore to force them up; and the Sticks must be heavier in proportion.

These Rockets are not used in common, but only for Curiosity.

In firing them, care to be taken to keep as far off as the long Stick and Portfire will allow, to avoid the Sparks of Iron catching the eyes or face.

METHOD of Fixing Rockets for Regulated Frames.

These are quarter pound Rockets loaded or Capped with Stars, having Sticks as usual.

The Frame consists of a Tin trough about an inch deep and twice as broad as the diameter of the Rockets.

In the bottom of the Trough, holes must be made for the Sticks to go through and the Rockets to rest on: these holes must be so ordered, that there may be sometimes one, then two almost close together at 3 or 4 inches distance from the Single one, then three almost close together, and so on according to the Artificer's judgment.

These Frames may be fixed at each side of a Building 12 or 14 feet square.

To fix the Rockets — take Quickmatch of only two threads, that has only been drawn thro' the first preparation, but no mealed

powder

powder sifted over it afterwards; lay them singly from end to end along the holes, securing the Match in proper places with small tacks not drove too hard; then put in the Rockets according to the holes.

Next fill up the Troughs with Bran, pressing it down with the fingers, not too hard.

It will be necessary to have leaders of Quickmatch to give fire by; and if thought proper, the four frames may be communicated together.

If carefully managed, the Quickmatch will burn under the Bran and discharge the Rockets regularly; but for greater security the mouths of the Rockets ought to be primed.

This Method is used, (amongst other Fireworks) to represent the small Eruptions from Mount Vesuvius, Strombolo, &c.

TOURBILLIONS or TABLE ROCKETS.

The cases are made of cartoon paper, pasted and hung to soak about ¼ of an hour, then Rolled up on the former and to have five or six turns under the Rolling Board to draw the paper close, a little paste to be put along the outward edge which is to be pressed close all along with the thumb nail, then the Case to be taken off and laid in a tray.

As these are pasted Cases, it is necessary to paste the body of the former all over, to get off the Case when Rolled.

The former is turned of Beech or Ash wood well seasoned.

The cases to be laid in a tray till they are about three parts dry, or half dry will do, then they must be choked close at one end and the choke secured with 6 or 7 hitches of middling packthread, then set the case with the former in it, on a large wood Block, and with 4 or 5 strokes of the

the Mallet set down the Choke, lay them when choked into trays, to dry thoroughly.

Remarks; the Cases must be so far dry before they are choked, that on putting the former into them the inside may not stick to or be made rough by the former; for which reason it will be necessary, after the cases have stood a day or two in the room to dry, to put them out in the open air in the shade, that the insides may dry equally with the outside; the due point of dryness must be carefully watched, for as they take some time in choking, were they let to be too dry at first, the last Cases would be difficult if not impracticable to choke.

Care must be taken not to Roll more Cases than can be choked in due time, which must be judged accordingly.

After

After the Cases are choked, they will require about a week in the open air to dry thoroughly.

All the chokes should be of equal length, which a little practice may attain without the help of a Gauge.

The Cases to be taken in doors every Evening, and at all times when likely to rain.

Summer is the proper season for Rolling fluted Carloon Cases, and it will be proper to Role a stock of each nature sufficient for 2 or 3 Years: about 20 dozen will do for Store.

When the Cases are thoroughly dry, they must be marked off in a Gauge, Fig.

Machine or Gauge for Marking off the Cases.

The principal point to be observed in making this Machine; is the exact setting of of the steel or iron points, these points may stand 1/10 of an inch above the wood, and are to be filed up after they are set in tight.

To use the Machine, take a case and put it into the Gauge, observing to turn the outward joint of the paper down upon the points, and the choked end of the case close up to the head of the Machine, then with a small Mallet strike all along the Case so as to get the impression of all the points; each Case to be marked off in the same manner.

After the Cases have been Marked off in the Machine, all the impressions on the Case must be retouched with pen and ink, as follows.

The Case marked off and retouched with

pen and ink.

Next

Next the Cases are to be Clayed exactly up to the first single mark from the choke — to do this take a half pound Rocket ladle and put a ladleful of Clay into a Case, then put in the long drift down to the clay, set the right thumb nail to the former exactly even with the top of the Case, draw out the former and measure from the thumb down the outside of the Case to see how high the loose clay reaches above the mark, if it is about half an inch higher it will probably drive down to the mark; if on measuring there is too little clay, put in more; if too much pour out a little; a little practice will enable to judge of this to a nicety, for some Cases, tho' rolled on the same former will take a little more Clay than others.

The

The Clay being determined, put in the former, and setting the end of the Case on a large wood block, give 21 strokes with a 13 Inch Mallet to drive down the Clay, then set the thumb-nail to the former, and drawing it out, measure; to see if the Clay is exact to the mark, if it is right, lay the clayed Case apart, and proceed in like manner with the rest.

If there is too little Clay, put in more, driving it down as before; if too much Clay, use a brass or copper scraper to take some out, till it is right.

The Cases being all exactly clayed, are to be put in Store.

The former and Drifts for these Cases must be turned out of well seasoned, clean, beech or Ash wood, all solid; the Drifts to have brass ferules on the ends.

Table

TABLE of the Nature and Dimensions of Tourbillions &c.

Nature of Tourbill.s	Cases			Vents for			Depth of Clay	Distances of			Size & Nature of Marroons
	Length Unchoaked	Thickness of Paper	Diam.r of Bore	Rising the Case	Turning the Case	Marroon		Rising Vent from the Clay	Turning Vent from the Clay	between each rising Vent	
Pounders	Ft. In. 10	In. 10ths	In. 10ths	No	No	No	In. 10ths	In. 10ths	In. 10ths	In. 10ths	Ounce
2	1:7,0	0,375	1,25	6	2	1	0,687	0,875	0,437	2,687	1
1	1:0,0	0,312	1,125	4	2	1	0,562	0,750	0,375	2,375	½
½	0:10,5	0,250	0,812	4	2	1	0,437	0,687	0,343	2,125	¼
¼	0:9,5	0,187	0,687	4	2	None	0,375	0,625	0,312	2,000	None

Nature of Tourbillions	Diameter of			Sticks			Saw for Tourbillions en Croix		
	Turning Vents	Rising Vents	Marroon Vent	Length	Breadth	Thickness	Diam.r of	Depth of	Length of Pins
Pounders	In. 10ths	In. 10ths	In. 10ths	Ft. In. 10	In. 10ths	In. 10ths	In. 10ths	In. 10ths	In. 10ths
2	0,281	0,281	0,125	1:7:0	1,0	0,25	2,0	3,0	1,75
1	0,218	0,218	0,125	1:0:0	1,0	0,25	1,75	2,625	1,25
½	0,156	0,156	0,125	0:10,5	0,812	0,187	1,282	1,968	1,00
¼	0,093	0,093	None	0:9,5	0,75	0,125	1,062	1,593	0,75

The Dimensions in the forgoing Table must be strictly adhered to in all points.

The Length of the Formers not set down in the Table for want of Room, are as follows,

2 Pr. length of Body 20 Ins. handle 4 Ins.

1 Pr. length of Body 15 Ins. handle 3½ Ins.

½ Pr. length of Body 12 Ins. handle 3½ Ins.

¼ Pr. length of Body 11 Ins. handle 3 Ins.

The Diameter of the Formers will be as the Bores of the Cases.

The Drifts must be very littler less than the formers in diameter, so as just to play freely in the Case.

The 2 and 1 Pounders require four Drifts each; The ½ and ¼ Pounders three Drifts each.

The longst Drift for each Nature, may be equal the whole length of the Case and the others gradually shorter, so as to take an equal length of Composition in Driving.

To

To Drive the Cases.

Chinese Composition.

	lb : oz.
Salt Petre - - - - - - - - - - - - - -	10 : 0.
Charcoal - - - - - - - - - - - - - -	2 : 8.
Sulphur - - - - - - - - - - - - - - -	1 : 4.
Prepared pounded Iron - - - -	7 : 4.

This Composition to be mixed exactly in the same manner, as directed for 2 Pounr Sky Rockets drove with Chinese fire. Page 130.

Size of Iron for each Nature: for 2 Pou.r N.o 2 & 3: for 1 Pow.r N.o 3 & 4: for ½ Pou.r N.o 4 & 5, the same for ¼ Pou.r

In order to Drive these Cases, there must be a large Block with Brackets to fix the Case in, exactly as in Page 33.d only sizing the Brackets to the Case; and the top of the Brackets must reach only to the upper cross mark on the case, on account of measuring to drive the composition and upper Clay exact.

General Rule. All pasted Cartoon Cases to be drove in these kind of Brackets.

Table

15.1

TABLE for Driving Tourbillions.

Nature of Tourbill.	No. of Strokes to each ladlefull	Nature of Ladles.	Nature of Mallets.
2 Pou.r	- - 31 - -	1 P.r	with a Pound Rocket Mallet.
1 - - -	- - 21 - -	½ P.r	D.o — or 31 strokes with a 13 Inch D.o
½ - - -	- - 18 - -	¼ P.r	with a 13 Inch Mallet.
¼ - - -	- - 15 - -	3 oz.	with a 10 Inch Mallet.

N.B. Two and One Pounder Tourbillions only, are used in the Laboratory; generally One Pounders.

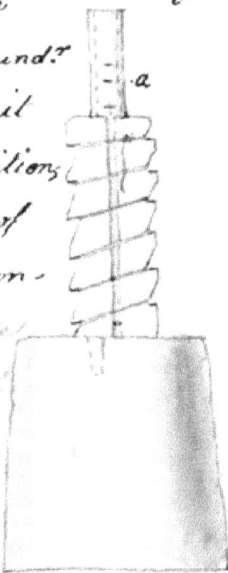

The Case Fixt for Driving.

The Case being fixed as in this Sketch; Suppose a 1 Pound.r take a ½ P.r Ladle and dip it full of the Chinese Composition; then with the small piece of Cane strike off the loose Composition even with the edge of the ladle, put the ladlefull of Composition into the Case, then the long Drift and drive down the Composition as directed in the Table, continuing one

ladlefull

ladlefull of Composition at a time, till the Case is drove exactly up to the Mark at a, then from the mark at a to the upper mark must be drove with Clay, answering to the other end prepared with Clay at first.

Each ladlefull of Composition to be struck with the small bit of cane, that it may be equally full each time; the shorter Drifts to be used in course as soon as they will reach the Composition; and the number of strokes to be exactly counted to each ladlefull of Composition.

All the Cases to be drove in the same manner as exact as possible.

The Cases being drove, the next step is to choke them close at the open ends, to perform this, the inside folds of paper must be loosened by thrusting a flat pointed pricker between all round down as far as the top of the Clay, about half the thickness of the Case, or a

little.

the pare must be loosened with the pricker without this method, it would be difficult to choke them.

They are then to be choked in the Choking engine quite close and as near to the top of the clay as they can be, and when choked, they must be tied down with good packthread in the usual manner;

When the Case is completally choked, set the lower end on a large block and give three or four strokes with the Mallet on the upper end to set down the last choke a little.

All the cases to be choked in the same manner.

The Cases being all choked, then the ends are to be pared equally into the shape of a button, with a knife, and being moistened a little with the mouth they are to be finished by beating them down with an 8 Inch Mallet.

The Tourbillion drove & choked at both Ends.

Clay .... Composition .... Clay.

In the next place, the Side Vents are to be marked off, which requires a Slip of Cartoon paper just long enough to go round a Case and meet; the breadth of this Slip must be exactly equal to the breadth between the end cross mark and the single mark next to it; a middle line must be drawn along the Slip and the whole length of the Slip divided into 4 parts from end to end, and the divisions pierced through with a sharp pointed pricker along the middle line.

The Slip of Cartoon paper markt off.

1 2 3 4

The use of this Slip is to obtain the side Vents at right Angles with the cross marks at bottom; the side Vents must be made reverse on account of working the Case round, and should turn with the Sun.

Application

Application of the Slip.

In this Sketch the Slip is placed for one end and secured by placing the thumb upon it, bringing the other end round the Case, with a prick, or mark into the Case at 1; then put the Slip round at the other end and mark it, but on the opposite side to the first; the Side vents of all the Cases to be marked in the same manner.

As some Cases will be smaller and some a little thicker than others, it must be allowed for, by shifting the Slip in proportion; it would be tedious to make a Slip for each Case:

The Cases are next to be Bored with a Gimblet of the exact size as given for the vents in the Table, page 151.

Third

First the four holes along the Bottom in the middle of each cross mark, are to be Bored, looking carefully every now and then to see that the Gimblet stands perpendicular all ways, observing to keep the Line.

The Gimblet must enter only so far, that the lower part of the belly or body next the worm may just go through the thickness of paper and only the worm to enter the composition, for which reason it will be necessary to take out the gimblet at times, to avoid Boring too far, when the Composition can be seen in the holes, or a little comes out upon the worm it is sufficient.

The side Lines are next to be Bored exactly in the same manner, only they must be at Right Angles to the four rising Lines.

As the boring with the gimblet raises the paper all round the holes when the cases are bored, take a sharp knife and pare off the rising of the holes even with the surface of the case, then with a small, round taper peg of beech wood, of the size of the gimblet, open all the holes fair and round.

To Prepare for Quickmatching the Rising Vents.

Take a case and with a sharp pointed pricker scratch the composition a little in all the holes, then take Cotton Quickmatch of 4 threads, cut a short piece and begin to prime one of the middle rising vents, put one end of the match into the hole and cut it off short, then make room with a round pointed pricker and put in another short piece, make room and put in a third short piece, the last must be a short piece doubled and forced in at one side with the end of the pricker, to keep all tight; both the middle vents to be primed with short match in the same manner.

The 2 middle rising vents primed with Quickmatch.

Then with the scissors cut off the ends of the Match close to the Case.

Next cut off a length of Quickmatch about an inch longer than from one extreme rising vent to the other, put one end of the length of Match into one of the vents and secure it well in with short pieces and the pricker, then bend down the Match gently along the Case to the other extreme rising vent.

Cut off what match at the end is more than sufficient to reach to the bottom of the hole, which must be judged, turn the end gently into the hole and secure it tight in with two or three short pieces and the pricker, then with the point of the scissors cut off the short ends of match at each hole, taking care not to injure the whole length in any part.

The Quickmatch laid along from each rising end vent.

All the Cases to be carefully Quickmatched exactly in the same manner.

Then

Then tear or cut out slips of tube paper, about an inch broad and the length of half a sheet: first paste over the Board a little with the large brush, then lay slips by one another singly, about six or eight, paste them over, then lay a fresh slip on each and paste them over; this is what is meant by pasted double tube paper.

The Cases being Quickmatched according to the foregoing Sketch; take a slip of pasted paper off the Board, and lay one end at the farthest mark beyond the Quickmatch, lay it all along over the Quickmatch to the mark at the other end, tear off the superfluous paper at the mark; then press down the pasted paper very close to the Case every where, and to secure the edges, dip the end of the finger in paste and rub the edges all along; the least opening might

spoil

spoil the effect, as the fire is exceeding sharp; As the Cases are pasted lay them in a flat tray to dry for two days.

The Case pasted.

a c b

At the same time that the rising tents are covered with pasted paper, it is usual to cover over the ends the same as in this Sketch, to make them look workmanlike.

When dry, they must be centered with a pair of compasses, to find the middle between a & b, making a mark with a black lead pencil as at C. care to be taken, in measuring not to prick too near the side of the quickmatch; the Cases being all centered, it will be necessary to describe the Sticks.

The Sticks are usually cut out of Ash hoops, and made exactly agreable to the Dimensions given in the Table; but as that does not shew their form, it may be proper to add a Sketch thereof.

Tourbillion Stick.

Now the Sticks are not flat, but have a regular Curve rising to about an inch at each end.

Curve of the Stick.

The Stick marked.

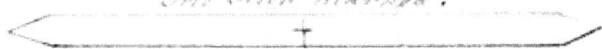

The Sticks must be measured with a pair of Compasses from point to point, and marked with a black lead pencil.

Next to tie the Cases on to the Sticks, tho' this is both facile and quick in practice, it will not be easy to describe without a number of Sketches; therefore, first place the Case upon the Stick, the Quickmatch downwards, and Center to Center; hold the Case and Stick between the fingers and thumb of the left hand; with the right hand take the end of a ball of fine packthread and put the end between the teeth, bring the packthread round the Case and Stick at opposite corners making four turns and pulling as tight as you

you can, at the fourth turn, bring the packthread under the case, close to the side of the Stick so as to as to catch the end packthread and secure it, take one turn round, then let go the end, and continue to make four tight turns at right angles over the first, at the fourth turn bring the packthread under the Case close to the side of the Stick, bring up the packthread and taking hold of the first end bring them together and make a tight firm knot, (not tying them directly in the middle at top) but a little on one side, then cut off the ends almost close to the knot.

The Cases tied on to the Sticks.

Front. Back.

From these Sketches, it may be easily inferred that

that the two cross Sticks are to stand at right Angles with each other; but a principal point is to keep the Quickmatch rising ends exactly upon a perpendicular to the plane of the Stick, Viz[t]

Section.

In this Sketch, I suppose the Case to be cut exactly thro' the middle, and thro' the middle length of the Stick, to show that the quickmatch must rest on the plane of the Stick; for if it inclines to either hand, the Rockets will not ascend in a perpendicular direction, but they will go to the right or left accordingly.

After the Cases are tied on, look along the back of the Case to see if the Quickmatch stands at right Angles with the Stick, if not, it must be rectified by turning the case accordingly, then with a flat pricker set the turns of packthread close together, and

at

at the bottom of the Stick; the cross should be made as exact in the middle of the Stick and Case, as the eye can judge, for it is upon this as a Center, that the Case and Stick turn when fired.

Next they must be pasted with double tube paper all over the packthread, over the cross at bottom and particularly at the sides between the case and Stick where it should be twice covered double; when pasted, lay them in a tray one and resting on the edge; that so the air may have recess to all the pasted part, let them Stand to dry for two days.

While these are drying, the Marroons for the top may be primed as follows, set a marroon on a block, and placing the point of a sharp pricker in the middle at top give two or three strokes with a small Mallet to make a hole into the powder, let the pricker stay in, then cut a length of

the

the smallest 3 thread Quickmatch, then take out the pricker and put in one end of the Match as far as it will go, cut it off at about an inch above the top of the Marroon, then make room with a round pointed pricker and put in another piece cutting it close off in this manner all the Marroons are to be primed.

The Marroon Primed with Quickmatch

The fixeting being dry; take a small gimblet about ⅓ or ⅛ of an inch diameter at most, then set a Tourbillion on the table and make a mark with the point of the gimblet exactly in the middle at top of the Case as nearly as the eye can judge, turn the Case and stick round to see if the mark is right all ways, then bore perpendicularly down a little at a time, 'till you find the gimblet just touches the composition, which may be easily seen by its bringing a little up upon the worm; all the case to be bored at top exactly in the same manner.

Next with a round pricker measure the depth of a top hole and cut the quickmatch of each Marroon to that length, at the same time cutting the match sloping to a point, to facilitate its going into the holes.

To tie or Fix the Marroons on.

Take a marroon and put the match fair into the top hole of a case; place the fingers below the case and the thumb at top of the Marroon to keep them steady in the left hand, then take a length of dutch twine, and holding the end between the teeth, take a turn round cross ways, at top of the marroon make a hitch and form the other cross, tying the two ends together near the top of the Marroon; then cut off the ends at about half an inch

from

from the knot.

Then see if the Marroon stands upright, if not, it **must** be set right; take another length of twine and give three or four turns round the cross between the marroon and top of the case, drawing them as tight as they will bear without breaking, then tie the ends and cut them off close to the knot.

Then dress the Marron again if necessary, and put the single cross of twine to rights at bottom of the sticks.

Fixing or tying a Marroon at top of each case in the same manner.

The Tourbillion with the Marroon tied on, this Sketch is as plain as I can make it.

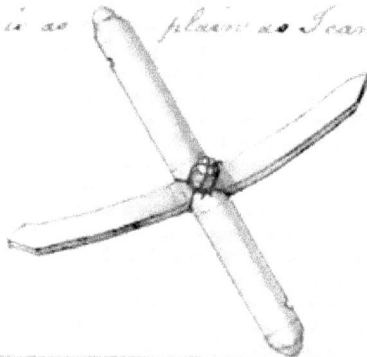

When the Marroons are all tied on, they must be pasted with double tube paper, going twice over the Marroon, and particularly at the top of the case and bottom of the marroon lay on three coats all round, one coat upon the other, well and close pressed every where; on the single cross of twine at bottom of the Stick, and on the sides of the case, once covering over will be sufficient; then set them in a tray to dry for two or three days.

In the mean time the Communications for setting fire to the case may be prepared; these are small leaders made of tube paper about $\frac{3}{10}$ of an inch in diameter: take a leader and measure from one side vent to the other, but rather take the whole length of the case for the length of the leader, and cut as many leaders to that length as are wanted; put a length of three thread Quick-

-match

Quickmatch thro' each leader, cutting the match off at about ½ of an inch from each end of the leader, then make room with the pricker and put in a short piece or two at each end, cutting them off almost close to the end of the leader.

The Loader Quickmatched.

Supposing the pasting of the Marroons to be dry, take a Case and a quickmatched leader as above; cut one end of the leader a little sloping, then put it into one of the side vents and bending the leader gently down, secure it with two turns of fine twine round the Case and leader near the vent; cut the other end of the leader to a slope and producing it to the other side vent put it into the hole, bend down the leader and secure it with two turns of twine as before.

Then bend the middle carefully together and tie them gently at the side of the

Case;

case; next with a pair of scissors cut out a small slip of the leader at the end of the double, so as to discover a small part of the Quickmatch; and lastly wind a small slip of tube paper round the double twisting it a little at the end, to serve for a cap, and they will be finished.

The Tourbillion fixt Compleat for Fireing.

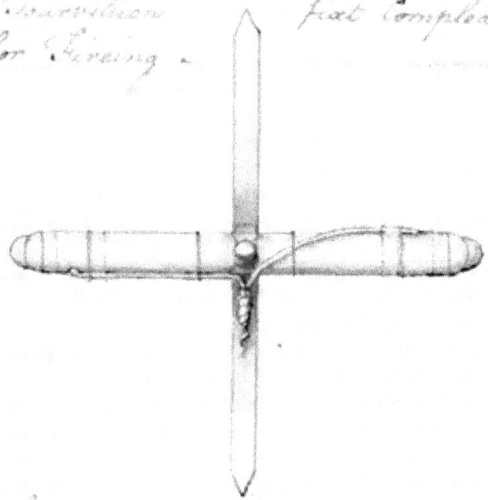

One thing should be observed, which is only to put a slip of single tube paper pasted, to cover part of the leader and side vents, both to finish and prevent accidents.

It will be proper in the next place to

to describe the Table for firing them upon, Fig.^d

Front.

Side.

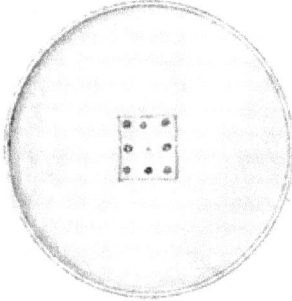

Table 4 feet diam.^r — Ash hoop round ¼ Inch thick; the Boards ¾ of an inch thick.

2½ Inc. deep. inside.

In the middle of the Table is a strong iron plate of 16 inches square, let in flush and secured with screws countersunk; the thickness of the plate ⅛ of an inch.

The use of the plate is to save the table, which would otherwise soon be destroyed by the fire from the Cases; on which account, the Tourbillion should always be set on the middle of the plate for firing.

To support the table there is a short strong triangle with a screw at top, about half

half an inch in diameter and a little longer, on which the table screws on, by an iron plate at the back having a female screw.

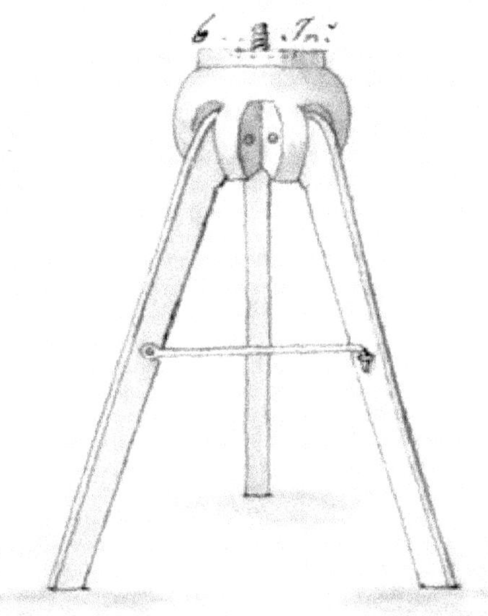

The whole of Table and Triangle when fixed may be about 3 feet or a little more.

Care must be taken in fixing or setting up the triangle, to see that the Table stands as horizontal as the eye can judge of it.

As two Tourbillions are usually fired at one time, it requires two Tables placed about 20 feet asunder.

There

There must be two people to each table, one to take off the case and place them on the plate; and the other to fire them.

When two fire together, one should give the Signal, that they may both keep time.

It requires a long Portfire Stick, and to retire quick; in order to avoid the Sparks coming upon the face &c.

The Table and Triangle fixed, with the Tourbillion placed ready for Fireing.

About two dozen 1 Pounder Tourbillions are sufficient for one firework, and they should be covered with a tanned hide to prevent accidents, and taken out by one at a time.

It may next be proper to mention the 2 pounders, and to explain the only difference, vizt.

Sketch of the 2 Pounder Case.

Now as according to the Sketch, there are six holes or rising vents, the 4 middlemost must be primed with short Quickmatch, and then a length laid along and secured in each end rising vent in the same manner as for those with 4 rising vents, only using 4 thread Quickmatch; in all other respects the work is exactly the same.

Tourbillions en Croix.

These differ from the others in construction and require some Explanation.

The

The Naves are usually turned out of Box or some hard wood, and have four pins set at right Angles; for the dimensions, see the Table at Page 151.

Nave for the Tourbillions en Croix.

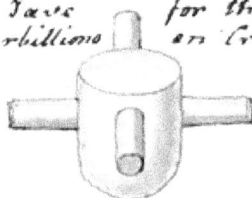

The Cases when drove, must be left open at one end to go upon the Pins, and each case has but one turning Vent, but the two opposite cases must have their turning Vents reverse; and the Quickmatching of the rising Vents is the same as before.

The cases are to be set on the pins with glue; the principal point is to set the rising Vents straight at bottom, which may be easily seen, by looking along two opposite cases, that the line of Quickmatch answers each other at right Angles to the bottom of the pins and center of the Nave.

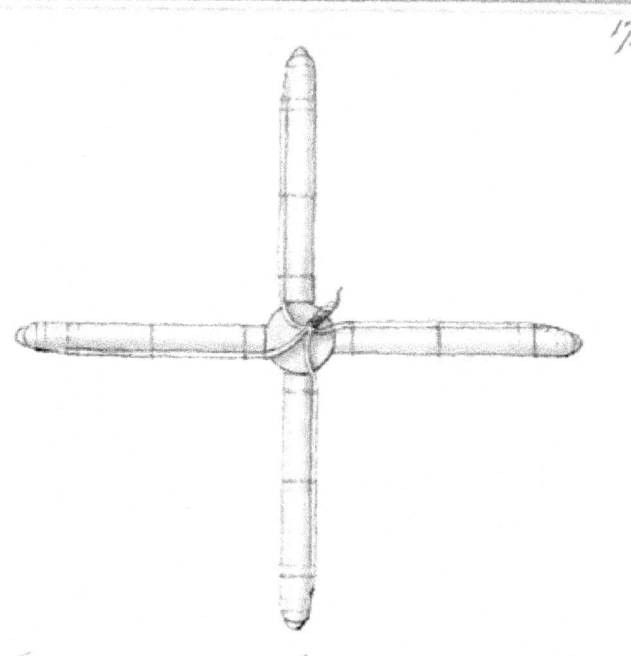

It is hoped that this Front or top Sketch of the Tourbillion as Cross-fixed, will fully explain the Method.

These are seldom used, but might, for Variety, be introduced in large works.

Care should be taken to keep Tourbillions at a proper distance from other works, as in rising they spread their fire to a considerable distance.

Tourbillions do not rise very high, but make a beautifull Show.

WATER ROCKETS.

These require to be managed with great care; as they are usually thrown into the water by hand.

There are four Natures, Viz^t 2 Pounders, 1 Pounders; ½ Pounders, and ¼ Pounders.

The Cases for Water Rockets are made of Cartridge paper and Rolled exactly in the same manner as for Sky Rockets, — excepting only two differences, One is that the Vent of Cases for Water Rockets must be exactly equal to ⅓ of the diameter of the Bore of a Case; the other difference is, that Cases for Water Rockets are very long, therefore the Body of the Moulds must be long in proportion.

The Case Rolled and Choked.

Dimensions of Cases, Formers, Drifts &c for Water Rockets.

Nature of Cases.	Cases.				Length of yarn for the Choke	Weight of Case.			Divisions		Sort of the Cases.	Length of the Former.	Length of Drifts.			
	Length cut out.	Length choked.	Exter. Diam.	Diam. of Bore.		Empty.	Drove.	Bounced.	No. of	Length of each.			No. 1.	No. 2.	No. 3.	No. 4.
Pou.ds	Ft. In.	Ft. In.	In. 10ths	In. 10ths	In. 10ths	lb. oz. d	lb. oz. d	lb. oz. d	No.	In. 10ths	of Bore.	Ft. In.	Ft. In.	Ft. In.	In. 10ths	In. 10ths
2 ...	2:0,0	1:9,83	2,25	1,5	1,75	1:1:0	2:6:4	2:10:4	16	1,0	1/3	2:0	1:8,5	1:4,75	13,5	9,5
1 ...	1:8,0	1:5,75	1,65	1,15	1,375		1:1:4	1:3:8	16	0,7	1/3	1:9	1:5,0	1:1,0	9,0	5,75
1/2 ...	1:4,0	1:2,0	1,30	0,875	1,00	0:4:4	0:9:8	0:10:12	20	0,45	1/3	1:6	1:1,0	0:9,0	6,0	4,0
1/4 ...	0:11,5	0:10,5	1,05	0,75	0,75	0:1:12	0:4:2	0:4:10	14	0,49	1/3	1:2	0:9,75	0:7,75	5,875	4,0

N.B. The Cases when finished must weigh no more than what is here set down, if heavier they will sink — — — — The Lengths given in this Table for the Formers and Drifts are the length of the Bodies only, exclusive of the heads which may be the same as for Sky Rockets.

It will be necessary, in the next place to lay down the Method of Marking the Cases and drifts for Driving.

N.B. those Divisions marked with P, signifie Powder; to distinguish them from the Rest which are drove with Composition.

Corn Powder for the Bounce oz. Dr. 3 : 8.

2 Pounder Wilder Marked off.

Corn Powder for the Bounce oz. Dr. 2 : 4.

1 Pounder Marked off.

Corn Powder for the Bounce oz. Dr. 1 : 4.

1/2 Pounder Marked off.

Corn Powder for the Bounce Dr. 7.

1/4 Pound Marked off.

These Sketches are intended to shew the Cases both empty and Cartrilated, at one view; which purpose it is hoped, they fully answer.

Next it will be necessary to explain the Method of Marking off the Drifts, of which one Sett may serve for an Example!

This Sett, answers to the Sketch of the 2 Pounder Case. Drifts solid Beech or Ash.

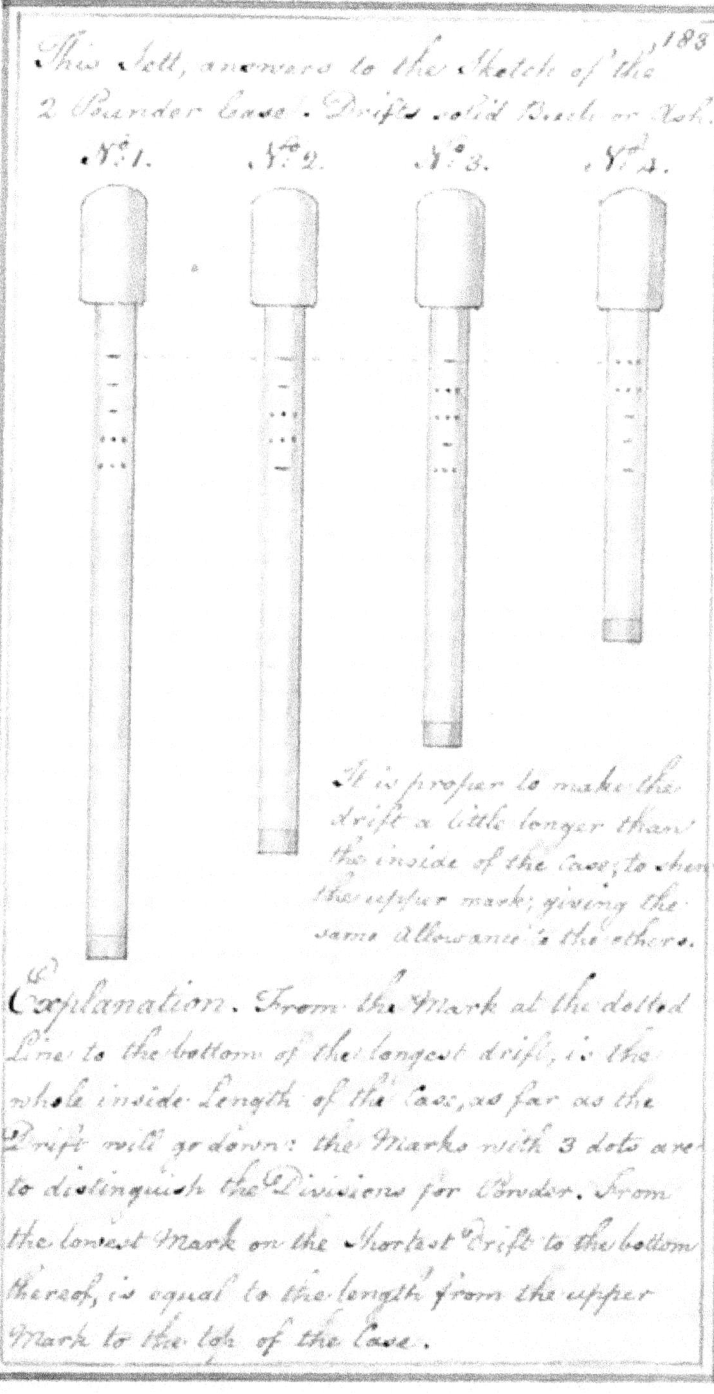

It is proper to make the drift a little longer than the inside of the Case; to shew the upper mark; giving the same Allowance to the others.

Explanation. From the Mark at the dotted Line to the bottom of the longest drift, is the whole inside Length of the Case, as far as the Drift will go down: the Marks with 3 dots are to distinguish the Divisions for Powder. From the lowest Mark on the Shortest Drift to the bottom thereof, is equal to the length from the upper Mark to the top of the Case.

From the foregoing Sketches and Explanation it will be easy to calculate and Mark off the Drifts for the other Natures; the ½ Pounder has 20 divisions, therefore each Drift must take five divisions.

Ladles, this is a critical point, for the Ladle must hold just so much Composition, as when drove down, will exactly fill up one Division; the Size of a ladle for the Composition and Powder may be found by driving a few ladlesfull of each, and when found the ladles should be tied up with their proper Drifts or marked: It is so many Years since any were drove, that the proper Ladles cannot be found; however I believe a Ladle that will contain so much loose Composition as will fill up to two divisions, will when drove down, about answer the purpose.

To make ready the Cases for Driving.

Take brown paper, tear it into small square pieces, and put a double piece into the mouth of each Rocket; thrusting it in with the end of the finger.

The

The foot or bottom of these Moulds, has only a start, and the Body of the Mould must be long enough to rise up equal with the highest mark on the Roce.

Foot or Bottom of the Mould, See Page 53.

Table for Driving.

	Strokes	
2 Pr.	31	with a pound Rocket Mallet.
1 Pr.	31	with a 13 Inch Mallet.
½ Pr.	18	with a 13 Inch Mallet.
¼ Pr.	15	with a 10 Inch Mallet.

Composition for Water Rockets.

	lb: oz. dr.
Salt Petre	4 : 0. 0.
Sulphur	1 : 8. 0.
Sawdust	0 : 2 : 4.
Charcole	0 : 2 : 4.
Mealed Powder	1 : 12 : 0.

To be rubbed together between the hands, then sifted all together 4 times through a hair Sieve.

Having

Having the Mould keyed tight to its foot, and set on a solid block; Cases; Drifts; proper Ladles; Mallet; Composition in one Box and Corned Powder in another, with the proper Ladle in each box.

First put a Case, (suppose a 2 Pounder) down into the Mould, then put in the long Drift and give three or four strokes with the Mallet to set down the Case, take out the Drift, and dip the ladle full of Composition (stroke along the edges of the Ladle with a piece of round Cane, to take off the spare Composition, that the Ladle may be equally full;) put the ladle-full of Composition into the Case, then the long drift, and give the number of Strokes with the proper Mallet according to the Table; then look at your Drift to see that the second Mark on the drift stands exactly even with the top of the Case, if so, the Ladle is right.

Then put in a second ladlefull of Composition; driving it down with the same number of Strokes and Mallet as before, then

then look to the Drift to see if the third Mark stands even with the top of the Case, which being right.

Proceed to put in the third ladlefull of Composition, driving it down as before, then see if the three upper dots for the Powder division, stand even with the top of the Case, then, take out the drift and put in the proper ladlefull of Corn powder and putting in the drift again, give only three or four quick gentle taps on the drift to set down the powder a little, then taking out the long Drift lay it by and take No. 2 drift.

Put in a ladlefull of Composition upon the Corn powder then No. 2 drift, drive down the ladlefull of Composition with the same number of Strokes and as hard as the first three ladlesfull; then look to your drift to see if the second Mark stands even with the top of the Case, if it is so, the Powder Ladle is right.

Then go on with another ladlefull of Composition and next a ladlefull of Corn

Powder

powder and then a ladlefull of Composition which being drove down, lay by No. 2 drift and take No. 3.

Put in another ladlefull of Composition driving it down; then a ladlefull of Corn powder giving only 3 or 4 gentle taps, next proceed with two ladlefull of Composition driving them down; lay by No. 3 and take No. 4 short drift.

Put in a ladlefull of Corn powder giving 3 or 4 gentle taps, then three ladlefull of Composition driving them down hard as at first, then the lowest Mark on the short drift should stand even with the top of the Case.

The Case being drove, take it out and put in another, observing exactly the same method in Driving the rest.

Only one Ladlefull of Composition must be put in at a time and drove smart; the Corn powder must have only three or four gentle taps and not be drove, for that would spoil the Effect; as the succeeding ladlefull laddlefull of Composition is drove down hard upon it, the powder is thereby sufficiently set, to answer the intention of forcing the Rocket under the water at each laddlefull.

The Rockets or Cases being all drove, are to be Bounced with Corn powder (the Quantity of which for each Nature of Rockets, is given with the Sketches of the Cases) — the Method is to set a dozen or more Cases upright in a box and put the proper Quantity into each, then three or four of the inward folds of paper are to be turned down upon the powder with a flat pointed pricker, then a short put in and two or three strokes given with a small Mallet just to set down the paper and powder a little,

All the Rockets being prepared with Bounces in this manner, are to be taken to the Choking Engine; there to be Choked, close at top, tyed down with packthread; the tufts at top pared, and beat into a button with a small Mallet; the Method

being

being exactly the same in all respects as described for Warning & Thunder Signal Sky Rockets; only Water Rockets should be choked as close as possible to prevent any Water getting in at that part.

Lastly, with a pricker take out the brown paper from the Cases and scratch the Composition in all the Cases a little,

Mix up mealed powder with spirits of wine to a middling consistence; and dipping the end of the finger therein, rub all round the inside of each Cup to prime them, then let them rest a day to dry.

Next having circles of tube paper stamped out equal to the diameter of a Case; with the finger paste all round the bottom edges at the mouth, and put a circle on each. when dry they may be put in Store.

The tube paper circles are to preserve from air, and outward Accidents.

The

It may be proper to hint, that the two first ladlesfull of Composition being drove a little smarter than the rest, will be a greater security against the Rockets bursting while held in the hand for Firing.

Methods and Caution for the Firing of Water Rockets.

1st. On a River it requires a Boat with three Men, One to direct the Boat, a second to carry the Rockets to the third who is to fire them; the Rockets to be kept at the Stern of the Boat well covered with a tanned hide or hair Cloth to prevent accidents.

— the Man that carries, is to take out the Rockets one by one as wanted, always covering the rest carefully up.

— the Man that fires them, first thrusts his finger through the paper circle, then holds the Rocket between the thumb and two forefingers of the right hand, as near to the mouth or Choke as he well can; then

sets

ets fire either with slow match or Port-fire, holding it about 2 seconds till he sees it is well lighted, then flings it as far from him as he can, continuing to fire one Rocket after another.

— The Man that directs the Boat, must keep a sharp look out, to steer the Boat clear of the Rockets, for should a large Rocket be suffered to approach too near, the attraction or suction would retain it; and the consequence would be a large hole blown thro the bottom or side of the Boat, by the explosion of the Burster.

One particular property of Water Rockets fired in Rivers is, that they always work against the Stream, which teaches to let the Boat keep down with the Stream.

These Rockets may be fired out of a Mortar, as many as the Cylinder will contain, with powder just sufficient to throw them to a proper distance, but then

they

they ought to be primed so, as to be sure that the whole will catch fire.

In Ponds: there must be a sufficient depth of water, 8 or 10 feet at least, otherwise the Rockets will stick fast in the Mud, and not rise again; it will be proper therefore to try one or two beforehand.

It is by no means prudent to hold the Rocket with a full grasp, particularly at the bounce end, as some are accustomed to do, for more purchase; for it is evident, that in case of an accident, the thumb and hand will be in great danger, whereas, by the first method, little damage can happen.

After all, if the foregoing Instructions are punctually observed there will be no more danger in Firing them, than would arise from handling an empty Case.

As several kinds of Prickers have been mentioned in the course of this Work, it may not be improper to give Sketches of Each, with their Use.

No. 1.

No. 2.

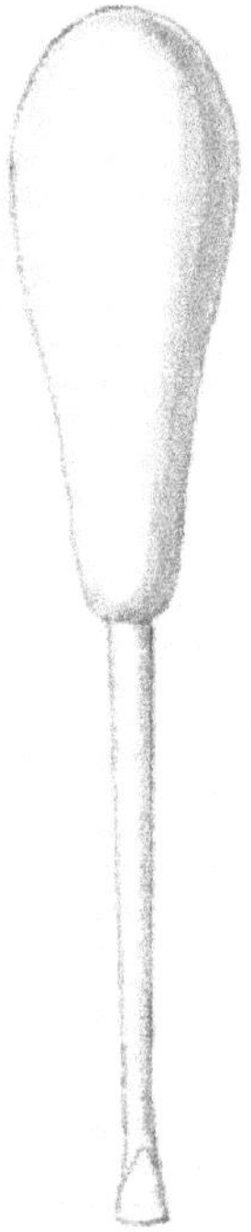

No. 3.

N.° 1. A round pointed pricker of which there ought to be three sizes, from the size of a Crow Quill at the point, to the size of a Goose Quill; the smallest are used for Priming two ounce Cases with quickmatch; the Middling ones for Priming three & four ounces and Tourbillions; the Large, for Priming Line Cases, Cascade Cases, Gerbs, and large Tourbillions.

N.° 2. A flat pointed pricker of three sizes, used for turning down the inward folds of paper for Bouncing and Choking of Squibs, 2 Pounder Signal Rockets; Water Rockets; and for opening or loosening the ends of Tourbillion Cases for Choking, after they are drove.

N.° 3. A sharp pointed pricker, used for scratching the composition a little in the mouths of Cases, to make them more sure of catching fire; and for boring thro the tops of Squibs [?] in order to string them for tying on the Leaders at Lots [?].

They should be made of good Steel a little tough.

Cotton Quickmatch for Fireworks.

Formerly Fireworks were Communicated with the Laboratory Quickmatch, which tho it answers the purpose in some Cases, is not in general so proper as the following.

The Balls of Cotton being at first only Single or of one thread; to make Balls of two threads, take the ends of two single Balls and wind them even together into one ball; for 3 threads, the ends of 3 single balls wound into one; for 4 threads, the ends of 4 single balls wound into one; for 6 threads the ends of 6 single balls, &c.

From this, Quickmatch is denominated of 2, 3, 4 or 6 threads, because it contains so many threads of Cotton in thickness.

— Particular care must be taken in winding the Cotton according to the above Size, to examine each thread, as you go on, in order to pick out certain hard, sharp, black or brown small particles from the threads

threads which ought to be freed from them as much as possible.

What these small adventitious substances are, I have not yet examined, but they cut as sharp as a knife; and therefore as the quickmatch must run thro' the hands, when reeling it off, it would be impossible for a Man to stand it long at a time.

About a dozen or twenty Balls of Cotton of each Size, may be wound and picked in readiness, it being much better to make a quantity; the work is slow on account of picking.

When any of the threads happen to break in winding, they must be carefully tied either with a weaver's or waterman's knot, and the ends cut off close.

Care should be taken to choose such single Balls as appear most uniformly spun and equal threads, as such will certainly produce the evenest Match.

The Balls of Cotton being in readiness, each

each size by themselves; we proceed to compose the Paste for Making it into Quickmatch.

Best red wine Vinegar — — —	3 Gallons.
	lb: oz.
Starch — — — — — — — — — —	1: 8. —

put about 6 Quarts of the Vinegar into a large Quickmatch copper pan, place it on the fire to boil, mix up the proportional Quantity of Starch with cold vinegar, and when the other boils add them together; and stir them well with a wooden Spatula; letting it boil about 5 Minutes.

Then let the pan be taken off, and the bottom dipt in cold water to extinguish any fire on the outside; let the pan be carried to some proper place out of doors.

While the vinegar and Starch is preparing, let a clean large earthen pan be got ready, (such as used for Crystalizing Saltpetre in) a large wooden Spatula; half a Barrel of mealed powder; and a wooden ladle to dip up the prepared vinegar.

First, a Quantity of the mealed powder

as 1/3 by guess to be put into the earthen pan, with a tin or copper shovel, then a ladlefull or two of the prepared vinegar, stirring them well together with the Spatula; adding more powder and more vinegar, stirring them well together 'till the pan is full, and the paste of a middling consistence, about the thickness of Tar; care must be taken to mix it gradually; to be done in the open Air.

This work requires three persons; one to attend the powder; a second to pour in the Vinegar, and the third, to stir and mix the paste well; when the pan grows full, the other two must assist to hold the pan, as it requires some strength to mix it then.

The Mixing finished; let the earthen pan with the paste and Spatula in it, be taken into a room, where there are three more earthen pans of the same size and clean; and 8 or 9 Bails of the prepared pickt cotton, all of one thickness of threads.

First with the Spatula cover the bottom of one of the clean pans about half an inch

thick

thick with the paste; take a ball of Cotton and unwind it in circular folds upon the paste at bottom of the pan, fold upon fold all over about half an inch high; then take the Spatula and sprinkle the paste all over the folds of Cotton, laying the paste at least ½ an inch thick upon it, and with the end of the Spatula chop down upon the composition and all over, to make it imbibe the paste well; then unwind again as before in circular folds all over the top of the paste, and about half an inch high; then go on with the paste and chopping with the Spatula, so continuing Stratum upon Stratum till the pan is full, letting the last layer be of the paste about an inch thick at top.

One pan being full, proceed exactly in the same manner with a second, and the same with a third.

One Ball of Cotton being nearly unwound, the end must be tied to the begin-

-ning

beginning of a second Ball so as to be sure that the knot will not slip; and when the second Ball is finished it must be tied to a third, as many as a pan will hold; tying the last end to the handle of the pan.

After the pans have stood two or three days to soak, the Cotton must be drawn between the hands into clean pans and if any part has not received the paste, it must be covered in drawing over.

A little of the paste must be put into each pan along with the Cotton; when the Cotton is all drawn over out of the three pans, it may be carried up to the Reeling Room and Reeled off.

This Work requires two persons, One to fix and turn the Reels.

A Reel being fixed, and the out end of the Match tied on at one end, the man that attends the pan sits down, and holding the Match between both hands, lets it draw

between

between his fingers, compressing it gently to make it as round as possible, the Reeling Frame must be turned round gently and steady, and the man that holds the Match must guide the turns of Match round the Frame as near as he can at about ¼ of an inch asunder, and when the Frame is full, break or cut the match, tying the end to the frame as at first, and leaving the other end hanging over the side of the frame.

The Frame thus filled, must be taken to the sifting table, and laid upon two Battens of Beech or fir, to keep the Match from touching the Table; then to be carefully sifted over on both sides with dry mealed powder, so as to leave no part of the match uncovered.

Then the Frame to be set upright and gently knocked once or twice upon the Battens, to shake off the loose powder from the sides of the Frame.

The

The Frame then to be set leaning against one end of the Room; and the table to be swept, and the powder put into the bottom with the rest.

In like manner, Frame after Frame, to be filled and sifted over with mealed powder, till the whole is Reeled off; and the edges of the Frames set leaning against one another, so as to leave free room for Air, and not to bear upon the main lengths of Quickmatch.

Then prepare more paste and more Cotton according to the Number of Frames, proceeding in all respects exactly as before for the whole.

After the Frames have stood a week in the Room, they may be set out in the open air in the Shade, to dry throughly for a week more.

When dry, the Quickmatch must be cut with a knife, on both sides all along the length edge of each frame, and the tops being gathered

together

together, and tied at top with packthread, leaving a loop to hang it up by.

Then each Bundle is to be weighed; tied up in paper; ticketed with its weight; and laid in Tin Boxes with sliding Covers ticketed, each size by itself for Store.

The Sizes and Pieces are by the Weights.

Uses.

Quickmatch of 2 threads is not to be Spun over with mealed powder after it is Reeled off; and is only Used for Communicating 4P.r Rockets for Regulated Frames.

3 Threads. For priming and communicating One and two Ounce sizes for small Trocanis, Single and double Vertical Wheels.

4 Threads. For all works in general above a 2 Ounce size; and even for 2 Ounce Cases in Rayonnant Fire.

6 & 8 Thread.. These are principally used for Experiments; but I believe that of 8 threads in Varnished Leaders, might be applied to the springing of Mines.

Index.

Fruiloni Wheel.

Single Vertical Wheel.

Sky Rockets.

Sky Rockets Continued.

Sky Rockets Continued.

Sky Rockets Continued.

Page.

Conclusion of the INDEX

to the 1.st Volume.

www.ingramcontent.com/pod-product-compliance
Lightning Source LLC
Chambersburg PA
CBHW030326270326
41926CB00010B/1522

9783337256050